IN A SHAKER KITCHEN

IN A
SHAKER KITCHEN

100 RECIPES FROM THE SHAKER TRADITION

NORMA MACMILLAN

SIMON & SCHUSTER

New York   London   Toronto   Sydney   Tokyo   Singapore

SIMON & SCHUSTER
Rockefeller Center, 1230 Avenue of the Americas, New York, NY 10020

Text and recipes copyright © 1995 by Norma MacMillan

SIMON & SCHUSTER and colophon
are registered trademarks of SIMON & SCHUSTER, INC.

Designed by Bernard Higton

Food styling and photographs © 1995 by Philip Webb
All other photographs see page 152

Printed in Spain

1 3 5 7 9 10 8 6 4 2

Library of Congress Cataloging-in-Publication Data

MacMillan, Norma.
    In a Shaker Kitchen: 100 recipes from the Shaker tradition/
Norma MacMillan.
      p. cm.
    Includes bibliographical references (p. 148) and index.
    ISBN 0-684-80110-8
    1. Cookery. Shaker.   I. Title.
TX715.Ml 66   1995
641. 566—dc20

CONTENTS

Introduction 6

———

SOUPS 30

FISH, POULTRY AND MEAT 42

VEGETARIAN DISHES 64

SIDE DISHES 76

BREADS AND BAKING 92

DESSERTS, PIES AND CANDIES 114

PRESERVES, SAUCES AND BEVERAGES 132

———

Shaker Communities 146

Bibliography 148

Recipe Index 149

List of Recipes 150

Acknowledgments 152

INTRODUCTION

> *Put your hands to work and your hearts to God, and benefits will befall thee.*
>
> ——
>
> MOTHER ANN LEE

It is over two hundred years since the founding of Shakerism in the United States. At its peak, in the middle of the last century, the United Society of Believers in Christ's Second Appearing had nearly 6,000 members, living in 18 prosperous communities that stretched from New England to Ohio and Kentucky. Today, numbers have dwindled to a handful, in one community in Maine, but the treasured principles of unity and simplicity still live on, as does the legacy of the Shaker cooks who labored with love and dedication to feed their Brothers and Sisters.

The Shaker movement began in Manchester, England, in the middle of the eighteenth century, with a group of Quakers who had been influenced by the radical and apocalyptical teachings of French Calvinists known as the French Prophets or Camisards. Meetings would begin in silent meditation, but then the worshippers would fall into trances and start to tremble or shake, shout or sing, and move about uncontrollably when they felt filled with the presence of the Holy Spirit. Because of this, they came to be called "Shaking Quakers" or Shakers.

Ann Lee (then named Lees), the illiterate 22-year-old daughter of a blacksmith, joined the sect in 1758. Four years later she married, and had four

SHAKER SISTERS AT ELIJAH WILD'S HOUSE, WHICH WAS THE FIRST TO BE BUILT AT SHIRLEY

children in quick succession, all of whom died in infancy. Her reaction to these tragedies was to become convinced that sex and marriage were the source of all evil in the world – violence, greed, disease, famine, poverty and all other forms of human misery – and that only by men and women remaining celibate all their lives, relating to each other innocently as brother and sister, and confessing their sins, could salvation be achieved. The other members of the sect came to share her views, and eventually she became the leader.

The Shakers were regarded with suspicion, even fear, because of their criticisms of the established Church and even more because of the religious ecstasy of their worship. Ann Lee was accused of blasphemy and imprisoned, an experience that had a profound effect on her. Upon her release she told her followers that she had had a revelation while in prison, and that the spirit of Christ had come upon her.

Her powerful conviction was that she was to be God's instrument to found a new and more perfect society on earth. She took the title of "Mother of the New Creation," and declared that she had had a vision of a chosen people awaiting her in the New World. So, in 1774, eight members of the United Society of Believers in Christ's Second Appearing, as the Shakers formally called themselves, including Mother Ann Lee and her husband, set sail from England.

This small group of Believers arrived in New York at the outbreak of the American Revolution. The first communal home, at Watervliet (then called Niskeyuna), New York, was built in the wilderness, and the new settlers had to work hard to sustain their bodies and their spirits. As in England, they were persecuted for their religious beliefs and practices as well as being regarded as English spies. Some colonists accused them of treason because they wouldn't take up arms in the War of Independence.

Mother Ann traveled and preached, hoping to inspire new converts, and the number of Believers grew. But the energy this required left her exhausted, and she died in 1784, aged 48.

At this time, the celibate Shakers, both individuals and families, lived separately, gathering on Sunday to worship. It was Mother Ann's successors, Joseph Meacham and Lucy Wright, who created the framework of communal settlements of Shaker "Families" that shared all work and possessions, with the aim of becoming self-sufficient. It began with all the Shakers in a vicinity assembling at the farm of one member, and selling all other landholdings. To the Shakers, this act represented a kind of separation from "the World," which is what they called non-Believers. The first community was formed at New Lebanon, New York in 1787, and by 1794, eleven communities had been established in New York and New England.

Before the dwellings and farm buildings were enlarged, this usually meant many heads crowded under the same roof. But because the Shakers were excellent farmers and worked hard, communities eventually spread over very large tracts of land, comprising pastures with flocks of sheep and cows, fields of corn and other grains, orchards of fruit and nut trees, woodlands, meadows, lakes and springs, acres of kitchen gardens full of vegetables and herbs, cow barns, hen houses, dairies, workshops, dwellings and meeting houses.

> *Do all your work as though you had a thousand years to live, and as you would if you knew you must die tomorrow.*
>
> MOTHER ANN LEE

In addition to the realization of the principle of communal property, Joseph Meacham and Lucy Wright established a structure of Shaker leadership. A hierarchy of elders and eldresses, deacons and deaconesses, and trustees – both men and women sharing equally in religious responsibilities – governed each Family, and a central ministry oversaw the community. The Shaker "capital" was at New Lebanon.

The Covenant, first drawn up at this time and revised over several years, can be seen as a kind of Shaker Constitution. In it the system of commitment to Shakerism was set out. Prospective converts could enter a "novitiate," to see if the Shaker lifestyle suited them. Once committed they gave up all their personal possessions, and whatever trade they had practiced in the World for profit – as blacksmiths, cobblers, tailors, weavers, bookbinders, farmers, and so on – was henceforth to be worked at for the good of the community. Signing the Covenant was meant to be a lifetime commitment, but it wasn't irrevocable: if a member wanted to leave, he was free to go.

The well-ordered framework of Shaker life was governed by rules or "Millenial Laws" that prescribed separation of the sexes, plainness and

ELDER HENRY BLINN AND HIS BEE HIVES, CANTERBURY SHAKER VILLAGE

neatness of dress, proper behavior, diet, education of young people, a complex system of job rotation, colors of paint for buildings, simplicity and absence of all adornment, set times for rising and eating, and so on. These rules were observed in all the communities, which made them very alike, despite the miles between them. With every aspect of life regulated, the Shakers were almost completely removed from worldly cares and pressures. Their lives were calm and peaceful, with their rites of worship being the opportunity to raise their voices and dance in praise of the Lord.

There were normally several Families in each community, and as communities grew and flourished, each Family could number as many as 150

Brethren and Sisters, although 50–100 was more common. Each Family lived together in its own dwelling, with men and women strictly segregated except at meals or in supervised meetings, and had its own fields, orchards and kitchen gardens. Members of different Families were not encouraged to fraternize, but came together for services and funerals and helped each other when required, particularly in business ventures.

The much-derided shaking, whirling and jumping that characterized the worship of the early Believers was changed by Joseph Meacham, to institute a more orderly service. Men and women sat on opposite sides of the room. Simple dances were performed in unison, the most common being stepping forward and back in a kind of march. Lively hymns were sung unaccompanied (over time, 10,000 songs were written, some original and some with words put to tunes "redeemed" from the World).

Mother Ann had prophecied that there would be a second Shaker revival in the West, so at the beginning of the nineteenth century, missionaries were sent out to the developing frontier. Over the next 20 years, nine new communities were established, in Ohio, Indiana and Kentucky as well as in New York.

By the 1820s a more corporate type of order had replaced the early, essentially communistic sharing of possessions and work. Shaker communities became very prosperous, due to their efficient production of goods that the World wanted and needed – dried medicinal and culinary herbs, garden seeds, fresh fruits and vegetables, maple syrup and sugar, preserves and fruit wines, eggs and cheese, handcrafted items such as brooms, straw hats and wooden boxes, and cattle in the western communities. Shaker-prepared goods, made with care from the

> *They have an extensive orchard, containing a great variety of excellent fruit, large medical and seed gardens, which are in fine order. These gardens are very profitable, as their herbs and seeds are everywhere sought after and purchased, being always esteemed better than any other which can be procured. They take great pains in drying and packing their medical herbs, and so highly are they valued that they have frequent orders for them from Europe to a very large amount.*
>
> FROM *PECULIARITIES OF THE SHAKERS*, 1832

best raw materials, had an excellent reputation, and the Believers had the added advantage of marketing their own products.

The Shakers enjoyed a quality of life that was better than most Americans could aspire to at the time. Even their animals were kept in spotlessly clean and pleasant conditions. However, the Believers still observed the basic tenets of simplicity and frugality and eschewed anything that was not useful (new technology, though, was embraced and even improved on). Food was one of their few indulgences, although the Millenial Laws of 1821 reminded members that they should be content with a "common" diet, and should not ask for anything special unless they were unwell.

Prospective members came to join the communities, attracted by the generous table and cleanliness and order of Shaker communities. (This caused tensions as older Believers thought only converts with sincere religious conviction should be accepted.) There were also "winter Shakers" who arrived at the onset of cold weather, stayed to partake of the plain but delicious fare, and other comforts, and then left in the spring when the hard work began again.

The Believers welcomed travelers and visitors and served them bountiful meals, as well as offering overnight accommodation and Shaker-made goods to buy. One sophisticated visitor to the Hancock, Massachusetts, community in the 1830s wrote that his meals were "worthy of Delmonico's." Other visitors, many of them famous, were not so complimentary. Charles Dickens spent a day at Mount Lebanon in June, 1842, and his first impressions used the word "grim" seven times. Other writers, such as Hawthorne and

> *There are no high cloister walls around their buildings, and no dark courts lead to their dwellings; but God's bright sunlight is invited everywhere, to cheer with its rays, this simple and unassuming people. The visitor or traveler will not find the forbidding words, "No admittance," written on any of their gates or doors, but meets with a kind and hearty welcome, with an invitation to examine and judge for himself; while hardly a day passes by in which hundreds of strangers do not come through their farms and villages.*
>
> FROM *THE SHAKER*, DECEMBER, 1871

> *Only a part of the Shaker people eat any meat at all. Many use no food produced by animals, denying themselves even milk, butter, and eggs. At Mount Lebanon, and in some of the other societies, two tables are set, one with, the other without meat. They consume much fruit, eating it at every meal.*
>
> CHARLES NORDHOFF
> COMMUNISTIC SOCIETIES OF THE UNITED STATES, 1875

Melville, were also disparaging, and Shakers were satirized in popular magazines. Even those who praised the Shakers for their industry found their religious practices bizarre and worthy of ridicule and their rules to be very harsh. Without doubt, though, the World was fascinated by the Shakers.

Material prosperity began to cause internal tensions among the Believers, with many, particularly the young, becoming impatient with strict rules in the midst of worldly temptations. Membership began to decline. Possibly as a reaction to this, in 1837, a revival of spiritual manifestions began, with Believers falling into trances, shaking and whirling as they did in the beginning, and receiving inspirational and prophetic messages from Mother Ann as well as the Apostles, the Angel Gabriel, historical figures such as Napoleon and George Washington, and Native American spirit guides. These strange occurrences quickly spread through all the communities, and carried on for a decade.

In the United States, outside of these communities, the early and middle years of the nineteenth century was a period of great change and upheaval, as the population almost doubled, there was a mass movement westward, and the country became industrialized and more urbanized. Food was abundant, particularly meat, and spirits were cheap and plentiful. So much eating and drinking caused a malaise termed dyspepsia, for which quacks offered all manner of cures. The temperance movement, which was then gaining momentum, wanted to reform the national diet too, to make it more healthy.

The Shakers shared these concerns, and many articles in their publications advocated a plain but wholesome diet containing plenty of fruits and

IN THE SHAKER VILLAGES, BUILDINGS WERE PAINTED DIFFERENT COLORS ACCORDING TO THEIR FUNCTION. WHITE WAS EXPENSIVE AND WAS THEREFORE RESERVED FOR SPIRITUAL BUILDINGS

Bread is called the 'staff of life.' Its importance in dieting cannot be over-estimated. The bread of a people determines largely the character of that people...Is the American superfine bolted flour the primary cause of national dyspepsia, and also of the loss of teeth?...After the wheat (which of all food contains all the properties, and in the proportions, of the component elements of the body) has been 'killed' in grinding, these elements are separated, and some of the most essential are thrown away entirely; the remainder is made into enervating, constipating, dyspepsia-creating, superfine white bread...

FROM *SHAKER AND SHAKERESS*, NOVEMBER, 1873

vegetables and whole-grain bread, eaten in moderation when hungry. For ten years (from 1837–1847), there was a ban on meat in Shaker communities, and rules were instituted against alcohol, tea and coffee. Not all Believers were in favor of vegetarianism, so in most communities there were tables for those on a "regular" diet and tables for those who preferred a "bloodless" diet. Temperance, too, was not strictly enforced, and by the end of the 1850s tea and coffee were again being drunk.

At this time, thousands of Americans joined religious movements that offered alternative lifestyles, including the Society of Believers. Most Shaker converts were evangelical Christians, but some were non-Christians who believed in the principle of a communistic society, while others were less spiritual Christians who were attracted to the secure and comfortable lifestyle. Charles Nordhoff, an American journalist who studied all the "communistic societies" in the United States at the time, including the Shakers, the Oneida Perfectionists and the Amana Society, gives a not uncritical account of the Shaker way of life then. He noted that Believers demanded hard work of their members, that some communities were more prosperous than others, and that members within Families could be from very different backgrounds. He also wrote: "In practical life they are industrious, peaceful, honest, highly ingenious, patient of toil, and extraordinarily cleanly." But "...they do not pretend that their celibate life is without hardships or difficulties."

After the Civil War, the population in Shaker communities continued to decline, due greatly to the increase in employment opportunities for men and the lure of the West. Initially, the Believers tried to keep up their numbers by adopting orphans and taking in poor children (many of whom left when they were old enough), but orphanages began to be established and living conditions were improving for the poor. As the general standard of living improved all over the United States, the unworldly and celibate Shaker way of life was no longer such an appealing option.

To attract new members, it was decided to relax some of the stricter rules, to allow music and reading as well as the planting of flower gardens. Attention was drawn to the sexual equality in Shaker life, to appeal to women, who at that time had few rights to property and independence (although, in fact, the only true equality was in the Shaker religious leadership). Worship was changed, to more closely resemble a Protestant church service, with no marching. Non-uniform dress was allowed as the twentieth century began, and the lifestyle became more like that in the World. More women than men signed the Covenant, and Shaker societies became increasingly feminized. The result was a reduced workforce, which meant that labor had to be hired and supplies bought in. Many of the once prosperous Shaker businesses could not compete with factory-produced goods and cheaper prices.

As at the beginning, the groups of Believers, mainly ageing Sisters, gradually gathered together, relocating to fewer and smaller communities and selling off furniture and land no longer worked. A once very prosperous national organization had shrunk to three small Families in New England, comprising 50 or so Believers, by 1947.

A GROUP OF SISTERS IN TYPICAL
SHAKER CLOTHING

Tis a gift to be simple.

In the 1950s and 60s, as the United States became increasingly affluent, a renaissance of interest in the Shakers began, helped along by a general religious revival. The rural Shaker communities seemed to offer a haven of peace in an ever more commercial world that was full of turmoil. Antique collectors and dealers became very interested in Shaker furniture; Shaker manuscripts and diaries were sought by libraries; composers such as Aaron Copland borrowed Shaker songs for their compositions. Devoted supporters bought and restored former Shaker communities as museum villages.

In 1959, Eldress Emma B. King, of Canterbury, New Hampshire, established a trust fund with resources from the sale of Shaker lands and assets, to provide for the remaining Believers as well as to preserve the Shaker heritage. In 1965, with only two communities of Shaker Sisters still in existence, she declared the membership rolls closed to new converts. However, Believers living at the other Shaker community, at Sabbathday Lake, Maine, were not in agreement with this, and the conflict caused the two groups to split. Today, in 1994, there are no longer any Shakers at Canterbury, but the community at Sabbathday Lake lives on, with eight members – two men and six women between the ages of 30 and 90.

Shakerism has changed with the times: Sisters no longer wear plain ankle-length dresses and bonnets, and Brothers cotton trousers and straw hats; they use computers and watch television; they take vacations and fly in airplanes. But they still aspire to unity and simplicity, produce goods that enjoy the same excellent reputation as their predecessors' did, and worship God in song-filled services. New converts are not sought, but there are about 50 inquiries each year about membership. As Sister Frances Carr said in a newspaper interview in July, 1994: "I don't think that God, who is in charge of it all, will let Shakerism simply come to an end. But at this point, I couldn't give you a clue as to how He or She will do it."

Shaker communities were always orderly and clean, with buildings and furniture constructed from local materials. Good ventilation and light were deemed essential, so buildings had many windows; floors were polished but not covered by rugs; walls of storage cupboards and drawers prevented there being any clutter. All was finished simply and unadorned, made solely to fulfill a function, as the Millenial Laws dictated, yet one imagines that the Shakers would have derived satisfaction from their good work even if they could not always admit its beauty.

The Shakers aspired to be self-sufficient, but, unlike the Amish, the Believers didn't eschew new technology. They were keen to try out every new invention, from indoor plumbing and electricity to telephones and cars, and they were always designing devices or improving on those they bought to lighten their labors and save time. They used the most up-to-date farm machinery, and were pioneers in the safe canning of fruits and vegetables. Among the inventions credited to them are an improved wood-burning stove, a washing machine, a means of making false teeth, a hernia truss, the first circular saw in the United States, a revolving oven, a dough-kneading machine, a water-powered butter churn, a "self-acting" cheese press, a mechanical apple parer, a pea sheller, and a fly trap.

Since the time that the Believers first offered their hand-crafted goods for sale, the World has coveted them. Nineteenth-century visitors to Shaker communities took away freshly baked pies, jellies, apple butter and applesauce, dried fruits, cucumber pickles, cured meats, fruit wines and cordials, honey, maple syrup and sugar, eggs, cheese, butter, and fresh

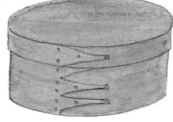

fruits and vegetables. Shaker merchants traveled far and wide selling brooms, straw hats and bonnets, jeans, wooden boxes, dried herbs and garden seeds. Today, genuine Shaker-made items fetch astronomic prices at auction, and reproduction or "Shaker-inspired" furniture and objects – including peg rails, multi-drawered cabinets and cupboards, and kitchen units – are very fashionable.

The Shaker seed wagon was a welcome sight in the last century. The Brethren had an excellent reputation as shrewd but fair traders who were honest in the advertising of their goods. The Shaker seed business began small, with the seedsmen selling locally, but it became a huge and very profitable industry. In many of the communities, whole fields were given over to raising vegetable seeds, and the Brethren experimented with hybridizing to produce new and better varieties.

Once the seeds were manually harvested and cleaned, they were packed into hand-folded and -sealed paper packages, which gave the cultivation instructions. (This was the first time seeds were put up in small paper envelopes in the United States.) At first the neat and colorful packages were printed by hand, but later presses were devised for printing them as well as "machines" for filling them. As the business expanded, seed catalogues were also printed, giving "recipes for cookery" together with the lists of available varieties. One list included six varieties of beans, six

> *Time lost can never be regained. After allowing yourself proper time for rest, don't live a single hour of your life without doing exactly what is to be done in it, and going straight through it from beginning to end. Work, play, study, whatever it is, take hold at once and finish it up squarely and clearly; then to the next thing, without letting any moments drop out between.*
>
> FROM *SHAKER AND SHAKERESS*,
> JUNE, 1874

The following seeds are selected with peculiar care, being the choicest kinds of the different varieties; and as such they will recommend themselves. They will be sold on the most reasonable terms by the pound, or put up in small papers for retailing, to suit the convenience of customers.

FROM A CATALOGUE OF GARDEN SEEDS RAISED BY THE UNITED SOCIETY OF SHAKERS, MOUNT LEBANON, COLUMBIA COUNTY, NEW YORK

varieties of beets, five varieties of cabbage, six varieties of lettuce, three varieties of melon, five varieties of radish, plus eggplant, asparagus, salsify, "spinage," sea kale, bell pepper, sage, summer savory, nasturtium and two varieties of parsley.

Growing, drying and selling medicinal and culinary herbs was another lucrative industry for most of the Shaker communities. In the late eighteenth and early nineteenth centuries, herbal remedies were widely used, and Shaker-made distillations, ointments, powders, herbal teas and other medicaments were in demand. They shipped medicinal herbs all over the United States as well as abroad, to Europe, Australia and even India (they are considered to have been the first to market medicinal herbs and herbal medicines on a commercial scale). Initially, wild herbs, roots, barks and flowers were gathered and sold; eventually thousands of varieties were cultivated in the extensive herb gardens.

Shaker Sisters used fresh herbs liberally in their cooking, noting that herbs turn even the simplest dish into "a fascinating, outstanding viand." They passed on that advice to the cooks in the World, in the leaflets that accompanied dried culinary herbs.

As with so many other Shaker industries, stiff competition from the industrialized world proved to be too great. But in the 1970s the herb business was revived at Sabbathday Lake, and herbs are sold today in their shop and through mail order.

A POSTER ADVERTISING SHAKER SEEDS. THE SHAKERS SHUNNED ORNAMENT IN THEIR OWN LIVES, BUT IN THE NAME OF GOOD BUSINESS WERE PREPARED TO USE STYLISH DESIGN

In the nineteenth century, life for the Believers meant hard work, whether in the fields, the workshops, the dairy or kitchen. All were industrious, unless they were ill, and each person had his or her appointed task. A set schedule ordered their lives, with the ringing of bells: all rose at the same time, gathered for breakfast at 6 am, started and finished work at the same time, had dinner at noon and supper at 6 pm, and went to bed at the same time. They were admonished to be considerate of others, to be quiet in their speech and movements, and to take great care with their personal cleanliness.

The Brothers and Sisters of a Family lived in the same dwelling, but in separate quarters and often with separate stairs and doors so they would not have any private contact. Men and women ate in separate shifts or at separate tables.

Although the Shakers professed to believe that women should have equal rights in society – and they invested God with both masculine and feminine attributes – all work was divided on traditional gender lines: women worked indoors at cooking, cleaning, sewing, ironing, spinning and weaving cloth as well as tending to the hen houses and dairies and filling the herb and seed packages; while men did more varied work in the fields and shops as well as traveling to sell Shaker-made goods. Of course, sharing the tasks would have brought men and women together, which might have led to irresistible temptation, and all work was seen as equal in God's eyes. But, as Lawrence Foster notes, in *Women, Family and Utopia*, visitors to Shaker communities often commented that the women appeared sallow in complexion and less happy than the men. However, there is little evidence in Shaker journals and diaries that anyone objected to the traditional roles.

A system of job rotation was followed, with each Believer, male or female, serving a set time at a task before moving on to another one. If an individual was very productive at a particular task, he or she remained there, and deacons and deaconesses stayed in their supervisory positions. Shaker Sisters served monthly "turns" in the kitchen, then moved on to the dairy or wash house; tours were also served in the weaving shop and herb house. Seasonal activities, such as maple-sugaring or fruit canning, brought all the Sisters together.

In the large kitchens, the Sisters worked in teams of two or three. Young girls served a kind of apprenticeship in the kitchens, helping the Sisters to

> *...tasks were cleverly allotted by the deacons and deaconesses so that if a certain sister and brother were supposed to like each other they were placed as far apart as possible. The general system was to have the elderly sisters near the young brothers while the girls were helping the older men...if a giddy young sister even glanced at one of the brethren she was sure to be marked by the watchful eye of Eldress Some One.*
>
> FROM AN ARTICLE IN *GOOD HOUSEKEEPING* MAGAZINE, 1905

prepare the tremendous amount of food that was required to feed the Family each day, as well as visitors and hired help. The kitchens were run efficiently, with each Sister having specific duties under the supervision of the deaconess who issued the instructions and doled out the supplies.

All was spotlessly clean, with whitewashed walls, well-scrubbed wooden tables and shining, polished pots and pans. There was efficient built-in storage for everything, and many kitchen utensils were fashioned of wood from locally grown trees: measures, scoops, bowls, mortars and pestles, and the familiar oval boxes that were used to hold everything except liquids. Enormous iron kettles, hung on arched, swing-away brackets, were kept full of simmering soups and stews all through the day, and huge ovens never cooled with the baking of so many pies and loaves of bread.

This hive of industry and activity, with its warmth and enticing aromas, must have been a favorite place to work. Certainly it drew in other Sisters and Brethren, because one of the Millenial Laws forbids anyone "to throng the kitchen or to go into it unnecessarily while the cooks are employed in it."

The Sisters who prepared the food also served it. The Believers gathered quietly in the dining hall, at the long, bare trestle tables set with plain white dishes. After kneeling for a silent grace they ate quickly, in silence, speaking only in a whisper if they wanted something. One Sister might read aloud: extracts from the previous day's newspaper, reports from other Shaker communities or a short story.

Each group of four people, or "square," had its own servings of food and condiments. All could eat as much as wanted to satisfy the appetite, but if

> *You will perceive that everything here is conducted systematically; the meals, labor, worship, recreation and sleep, all succeed in such regular order, that one thing never interferes with another. Consequently, the members all acting together in concert, and all endeavoring to promote each other's happiness, perform a great amount of labor, without any individual appearing to make very great exertion...*
>
> FROM *PECULIARITIES OF THE SHAKERS*, 1832

you took something onto your plate you finished it (except for bones and inedible skins). Nothing was to be wasted – you "Shakered" your plate.

Early Shaker cooking was very plain and frugal fare, but as the communities prospered, food became plentiful and varied. Meals were simple but wholesome and delicious, made from the freshest fruits and vegetables in season or home-canned produce, rich cream and butter from the dairy, home-reared meat and freshly caught fish, eggs from the hen house, breads of all kinds leavened with yeast from home-grown hops, and herbs gathered that morning from the gardens. As noted by a Sister Marcia in *Good Housekeeping* magazine in 1905: "On the ordinary farm the choicest of everything goes to market, while in a Shaker Village the vegetables, cream, meats, etc. are used at home."

The kitchen Sisters were thrifty and inventive, and were always looking for new ideas and inspiration. Just as with cooks in the World, they clipped recipes from magazines and newspapers, and wrote them by hand in their journals. They shared them with their fellow Sisters, too. The monthly periodical of the Society of Believers, published between 1871 and 1899 (first called *The Shaker* and later *Shaker and Shakeress*, *The Shaker Manifesto* and, finally, *The Manifesto*), included many recipes and household hints, as well as articles from correspondents on food and healthy eating. There were also recipes in a series of almanacs printed from 1882 to 1884.

Shaker recipes usually gave precise weights and measures, although these were sometimes unusual: "butter the size of a horse chestnut" or enough

> *See that your house is kept clean and your victuals are prepared in good order, that when the brethren come in from their hard work they can bless you, and eat their food with thankfulness, without murmuring, and be able to worship in the beauty of holiness...let your words be few, and seasoned with grace.*
>
> MOTHER ANN LEE

A MODERN INTERPRETATION OF A SHAKER KITCHEN

cream to fill a particular bowl. Other recipes might be just lists of ingredients without directions.

In 1882, *Mary Whitcher's Shaker House-Keeper* appeared, the only Shaker cookbook published in the nineteenth century. It contained 150 recipes, plus menus for each day of the week. The book advertised medicines, especially the merits of the sarsaparilla syrup produced by the Canterbury Shakers, and was given away.

❧

This is a collection of recipes inspired by the cooking of the Shakers in the last century. The skills and achievements of the kitchen Sisters represent the best of American country cooking: plain and simple fare that is wholesome and natural, seasonal and abundant, but above all delicious. Methods used in this book are modern; now unfashionable ingredients have been replaced; and quantities of butter and cream have been reduced. But the old-fashioned virtues embodied by the Shaker kitchen will always remain.

A FEW NOTES ON INGREDIENTS AND MEASUREMENTS

For the best results, use only the freshest ingredients, produced as naturally as possible: eggs from free-range chickens, sweet unsalted butter, real maple syrup, pure vanilla extract, pressed apple cider and fresh herbs.

In a few recipes, hard alcoholic cider is called for; fresh "sweet" cider can be substituted, but try to choose one pressed from a tart variety of apple.

> *All meals should be eaten calmly and deliberately and as pleasantly as possible.*
>
> FROM *THE MANIFESTO*, NOVEMBER, 1880

If fresh herbs are not available, dried can be substituted in most cases. Use one-third the quantity given.

Recipes have been tested using large eggs and all-purpose flour (unless otherwise specified). Flour was measured by scooping in the cup or spoon and then leveling off.

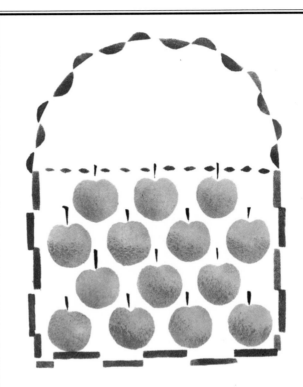

What we deem goodly order we're willing to state,
Eat hearty and decent, and clean out our plate;
Be thankful to heaven for what we receive,
And not make a mixture or compound to leave

We find of those bounties which heaven does give,
That some live to eat, and that some eat to live;
That some think of nothing but pleasing the taste,
And care very little how much they do waste.

FROM A TABLE "MONITOR" POSTED IN THE DINING ROOM

CHAPTER ONE

SOUPS

Huge pots of stock, made from bones, trimmings and the cooking water from vegetables, simmered all day long and were used for nourishing soups — creamy chowders, smooth vegetable soups, broths with rice, and clear soups with vegetables and herbs. In the early days, soup often formed the main part of the meal at supper, with bread and butter, cheese and stewed fruit.

Spring Vegetable and Herb Soup

The first young vegetables and herbs of spring were eagerly awaited after a long winter of cellared root vegetables, salted meats, dried fruits and other preserves.

4–6 SERVINGS

6 ounces baby carrots (about 2 dozen), scrubbed or peeled
6 ounces baby leeks or scallions (about 8) or use pearl onions
1 tablespoon butter
2 medium-size celery stalks, sliced
5 cups good vegetable or chicken stock, preferably homemade
5 ounces baby zucchini (about 4), sliced
a large strip of lemon zest
2 teaspoons fresh thyme leaves
1 cup shelled fresh or frozen green peas
4 leaves of Boston lettuce, shredded
a handful of sorrel or baby spinach leaves, shredded
salt and pepper

Leave the carrots whole. Cut leeks or scallions into pieces the same length as the carrots.

Melt the butter in a heavy saucepan and add the carrots, onions and celery. Cover and cook over a low heat for 5 minutes, stirring occasionally.

Pour in the stock and bring to a boil. Add the zucchini, lemon zest and thyme. Reduce the heat and leave to simmer until the vegetables are just tender, 20–30 minutes.

Meanwhile, blanch fresh peas in boiling salted water for 2 minutes. Drain and refresh under cold running water. If using frozen peas, put them in a strainer and pour boiling water over them to thaw. Drain well.

Add the peas, lettuce and sorrel or spinach to the soup. Season with salt and pepper. Simmer for a further 1 minute. Discard the lemon zest and serve hot.

Fresh Corn Chowder

Manuscript recipes for fresh corn chowder were much richer than the modern version here: they used all cream and much more butter.

4 SERVINGS

4–6 ears of corn (to make 2 cups kernels)
2 tablespoons butter
2 tablespoons flour
3½ cups milk, or 1¾ cups milk plus 1¾ cups chicken stock
1–2 whole cloves
1 small onion, peeled
½ cup heavy cream
a pinch of sugar
salt and pepper

Shuck the corn. With a sharp knife, cut the kernels from the cobs. Hold each cob upright in a shallow dish and scrape lengthwise with the back of the knife to remove all the corn "milk." Set the kernels and corn milk aside.

Melt the butter in a heavy saucepan and stir in the flour. Cook, stirring, 2–3 minutes. Gradually stir in the milk or milk and stock. Bring to a boil, stirring. Stick the cloves into the onion and add to the pan. Simmer 5 minutes.

Add the corn kernels and corn milk. Stir in the cream. Add the sugar and season to taste. Bring back to a boil.

Reduce the heat to low and simmer gently until the corn is tender but still firm, about 30 minutes.

Discard the clove-studded onion. Taste the chowder for seasoning and serve very hot.

COOK'S NOTE If you prefer the corn to be softer in texture, blanch the kernels in boiling salted water for 2–3 minutes first.

SPICY BAKED BEAN SOUP

Nourishing and sustaining baked beans were a staple food in Shaker communities, just as they were in households in the World. Thus, there were always leftover beans, and the inventive Shaker Sisters devised soups and other dishes to use them up.

4–6 SERVINGS

1 tablespoon vegetable oil
1 small yellow onion, chopped
1–2 celery stalks, chopped
3 cups homemade slow-baked beans (page 85)
4 cups water
1 can (16-ounce) crushed tomatoes in tomato purée
or stewed tomatoes
¼ teaspoon dried hot red pepper flakes
salt and pepper

Heat the oil in a heavy saucepan, add the onion and celery and cook, stirring, until soft. Add the baked beans, water and tomatoes and stir well to mix. Add the pepper flakes. Bring to a boil, then cover and let simmer 30 minutes.

Ladle the soup into a food processor and work until quite smooth, then rub it through a strainer into a clean saucepan. Alternatively use a food mill. Season with salt and pepper. Reheat the soup and serve hot.

POTATO AND LEEK SOUP

The "pot liquor," or cooking water from vegetables, was never wasted, but was saved for soups, gravies and sauces, as well as for cooking noodles and dumplings. Here the caraway-infused potato pot liquor provides the base for a thick, hearty soup, which has a really good potato flavor. The recipe is based on one in *Mary Whitcher's Shaker House-Keeper*.

8 SERVINGS

3 pounds potatoes, all about the same size
1½ tablespoons caraway seeds
1 bay leaf
salt and pepper
3 medium-size leeks, total weight about 1 pound,
trimmed and finely chopped
2 cups light cream, or 1 cup milk plus 1 cup
light cream
1 tablespoon chopped fresh thyme

Scrub the potatoes but don't peel them. Put them in a large saucepan with the caraway seeds, bay leaf and a large pinch of salt. Cover with plenty of cold water. Bring to a boil, then reduce the heat and simmer until the potatoes are just tender when pierced with the tip of a knife, about 20 minutes.

Drain the potatoes in a colander set in a bowl, and set them aside to cool. Strain the cooking liquid and reserve 6 cups.

When the potatoes are cool enough to handle, peel them and chop coarsely. Put them back in the saucepan with the reserved strained liquid. Add the leeks. Bring to a boil and simmer gently until the leeks are soft, about 30 minutes.

Ladle the soup into a food processor and work until quite smooth but still with some texture. Return to the pan and stir in the cream and thyme. Season with salt and pepper. Reheat without boiling. Serve hot.

OVERLEAF: FRESH CORN CHOWDER (LEFT), CREAM OF SQUASH SOUP

CREAM OF SQUASH SOUP

The Native Americans introduced the first European settlers to pumpkin and other winter squashes. These useful vegetables could be harvested in the fall and kept through the winter, thus being available to make warming soups and pie fillings. In early Shaker manuscripts pumpkin was called "pompoon," which probably came from "pompion" or "pumpion," a word used by the English in the seventeenth century.

6 SERVINGS

1 3-pound piece of pumpkin, or use butternut or
other winter squash
2 tablespoons butter
1 yellow onion, minced
5 cups good chicken stock, preferably homemade
1 teaspoon grated orange zest
2 teaspoons minced fresh ginger or ½ teaspoon
ground ginger
salt and pepper

Preheat the oven to 400°F.

Scoop the seeds and fibers out of the piece of pumpkin (if using butternut squash, cut it lengthwise in half first). Put the squash, cut side down, on a lightly oiled baking sheet. Bake until soft and collapsed, 50–60 minutes. Let the squash cool slightly, then remove and discard the skin, scraping off all the flesh onto the baking sheet. Set aside.

Melt the butter in a heavy saucepan. Add the onion, cover and cook over a very low heat until soft but not colored, stirring occasionally. Add the pumpkin flesh with any juices on the baking sheet and mash it coarsely with a fork or spoon. Pour in the stock and add the orange zest and ginger. Season with salt and pepper. Bring to a boil, then cover, reduce the heat and let simmer 25–30 minutes.

Pour the soup into a food processor and work until smooth, then press through a fine strainer back into the saucepan. (If using butternut squash, you will not need to strain the soup after processing it.) Alternatively, use a food mill. Reheat briefly and check the seasoning before serving.

BEEF AND VEGETABLE SOUP

Frugal homemakers of the last century never discarded meat bones and trimmings, and the Shaker Sisters were no exception to this golden rule of good housekeeping. Bones were used to make bouillons and stocks to form the base for hearty soups.

8–10 SERVINGS

*3 pounds meaty beef soup bones or use sliced beef
shank or neck
1 veal knuckle (optional)
2½ quarts water
2 large onions, chopped
2 large celery stalks, chopped, plus leaves if available
1 handful of parsley sprigs
1 small handful of fresh thyme sprigs
1 bay leaf
12 black peppercorns, slightly crushed with the side
of a knife
2 whole cloves
3 carrots, diced
1 medium-size turnip, diced
2–3 boiling potatoes, diced
1 cup shredded cabbage
1 can (16-ounce) butter beans, drained
salt and pepper*

Put the bones in a large pot or kettle and pour in the water. Bring to a boil, skimming off the foam that rises to the surface. When the foam has stopped rising, add half the onion and celery. Reserve a few sprigs of parsley and thyme and add the remainder to the pot with the bay leaf, peppercorns and cloves. Reduce the heat, cover and let simmer 3–3½ hours.

Remove the bones from the pot and set aside. Strain the bouillon through a colander set in a large bowl, then pour it through a fine strainer back into the pot.

Add the remaining onion and celery to the bouillon together with the diced vegetables. Bring to a boil, then simmer gently about 30 minutes.

Meanwhile, take the meat from the bones and cut it into small chunks. Chop the reserved herbs.

Add the meat, chopped herbs, cabbage and butter beans to the soup. Season with salt and pepper. Simmer until all the vegetables are tender, about 5 minutes more. Serve hot, with herb bread or biscuits.

COOK'S NOTE If you can, let the strained bouillon cool, then lift off the layer of fat that will set on the surface.

OLD-FASHIONED CHICKEN SOUP WITH NOODLES

The chickens raised by Shaker communities in the last century would have had much more flavor than the birds we buy today, as their varied diet included the greens and bugs they foraged for themselves. The flocks were large, and mature laying hens and old roosters would have ended up in the soup pot. If you can find a stewing chicken, by all means use it for this soup. Otherwise, choose a free-range chicken.

6–8 SERVINGS

1 3- to 3½-pound chicken, ideally a stewing hen, cut
in pieces
3 large leeks, total weight about 1½ pounds
1 large sprig of fresh rosemary
a few sprigs of fresh parsley
1 bay leaf
2½ quarts water
1 celery stalk, cut in ¾-inch pieces
2–3 carrots, cut in ½-inch slices
2 parsnips, cut in ½-inch slices
salt and pepper
1 large handful of fresh homemade noodles (page 88)

Put the chicken pieces in a large pot or kettle. Cut the green tops off the leeks and chop coarsely. Set the white parts aside. Add the green tops to the pot with the herbs and pour in the water. Bring to a boil, skimming off the foam that rises to the surface. Reduce the heat to low, cover and let simmer until the chicken is very tender, 1–1½ hours (a stewing hen will take longer to cook).

Lift out the chicken pieces and set them aside. Strain the stock through a colander set in a bowl, then pour it through a fine strainer back into the pot. Skim off the fat from the surface of the stock. (If you have time, let the stock cool and then refrigerate it; the fat will set on the surface and can be lifted off.)

Cut the white parts of the leeks in ½-inch slices and add to the stock with the celery, carrots and parsnips. Season with salt and pepper. Bring to a boil, then partially cover the pot and simmer 20 minutes.

Meanwhile, remove the chicken meat from the bones, discarding all the skin and fat. Coarsely shred as much of the meat as you want for the soup; keep the remainder for sandwiches or salads.

Add the noodles to the soup. Bring back to a boil and cook about 5 minutes or until just tender.

Add the shredded chicken meat to the soup just before the end of the noodles' cooking time. Check the seasoning before serving.

COOK'S NOTE If you prefer, use 3 ounces dried wide egg noodles, and cook for the time given on the package.

FISH CHOWDER

When first made in New England, chowders were very thick fish dishes, but by the nineteenth century they had become thick, chunky soups. Many Shaker recipes used cracker meal for thickening chowders.

6 SERVINGS

4 pounds white fish such as cod, haddock or hake,
filleted, bones and trimmings reserved
3 large yellow onions, halved and sliced
2 whole cloves
1 slice of lemon
4½ cups water
¼ pound salt pork or thick-cut bacon, diced
1½ pounds boiling potatoes, diced
2 cups whole milk
1–2 tablespoons butter
salt and pepper
soda crackers to serve

Skin the fish fillets and cut in ¾-inch chunks; set aside.

PREVIOUS PAGES: OLD-FASHIONED CHICKEN SOUP WITH NOODLES

Put the fish bones and trimmings in a heavy saucepan and add one of the sliced onions, the cloves and lemon slice. Pour in the water. Bring to a boil, then reduce the heat and let simmer gently 20 minutes.

Strain the fish stock through a colander set in a large bowl, then pour it through a fine strainer. Reserve 4 cups of the stock.

Put the salt pork or bacon in a large pot or kettle and cook over a low heat until the fat is rendered and the pork or bacon is browned. Lift out the browned bits with a slotted spoon and drain on paper towels. Pour most of the fat from the pot, leaving just a film.

Add the remaining onions to the pot and cook, stirring, until they are soft. Add the potatoes and stir to mix with the onions. Cook 3–4 minutes, stirring occasionally. Pour in the fish stock and bring to a boil. Reduce the heat to low, cover and simmer until the potatoes are just tender, about 15 minutes.

Stir in the milk and bring back to a boil. Add the fish. Cook gently, uncovered, until the fish is opaque, about 5 minutes.

Return the browned salt pork or bacon to the pot. Add the butter and season with salt and pepper. Heat through gently without boiling. Serve hot.

COOK'S NOTE If you prefer a thicker chowder, before adding the fish use a spoon or fork to mash some of the potato against the side of the pan.

OYSTER STEW

Many ingredients that are expensive today were commonplace and cheap in the eighteenth and nineteenth centuries, oysters being a good example. When they were in season, in fall and winter, oysters appeared often on Shaker tables, fried or used in soups, stews and pies, and were thought to be very nutritious. The recipe here is based on one from *Mary Whitcher's Shaker House-Keeper.*

6 SERVINGS

3 dozen fresh oysters
6 tablespoons butter
⅛ teaspoon cayenne
2½ cups whole milk, warmed
1½ cups heavy cream, warmed
salt and white pepper

Shuck the oysters and add them to a saucepan with all their liquid. Add the butter and cayenne. Cook over a low heat for 3–4 minutes or until the oysters are just firm and the edges are starting to curl.

Add the milk and cream and stir to mix. Season with salt and pepper. Cook for a further 1–2 minutes. Serve immediately.

COOK'S NOTE Sprinkle with chopped fresh chives or parsley if desired.

CHAPTER TWO

FISH, POULTRY AND MEAT

Meat was originally eaten at breakfast, later at midday dinner. The western communities raised herds of cattle, while eastern ones had dairy cattle and flocks of sheep. All communities had pigs and chickens, kept in clean, well-ventilated conditions, and fresh fish was caught in ponds and lakes. Before refrigeration fresh meat had to be eaten as quickly as possible, or it was salted, smoked or used to make sausage or head cheese.

FISH AND EGGS

In *The Best of Shaker Cooking,* Amy Bess Miller and Persis Fuller note that this dish of fish, eggs and rich milk or cream was a favorite in all Shaker communities. Mary Whitcher gives a recipe using salted codfish and cream, and garnishes it with chopped hard-boiled egg. The recipe here combines smoked and fresh fish, for a particularly delicious flavor.

4–6 SERVINGS

½ pound fresh cod fillet
½ pound finnan haddie (smoked haddock fillet) or other smoked fish
2 cups rich whole milk or 1 cup milk plus 1 cup light cream
1 slice of onion
1 bay leaf
a few black peppercorns
1–2 tablespoons butter
salt and pepper
2 pounds potatoes, cooked and thinly sliced
4 hard-boiled eggs, sliced

Preheat the oven to 350°F.

Put the cod and finnan haddie in a shallow baking dish and add the milk or milk and cream mixture, onion slice, bay leaf and peppercorns. Cover the dish with a lid or foil and put it in the oven. Poach the fish until it is just firm and will almost flake, 15–20 minutes.

Remove the fish to a plate. Strain the poaching milk through a fine strainer set in a bowl. Add the butter and season with salt and pepper. When the fish is cool enough to handle, break it into large flakes, discarding any skin and bones.

Wipe out the baking dish and butter it. Make a layer of potato slices on the bottom. Scatter over a layer of fish and cover with a layer of egg slices. Repeat the layers until the ingredients are used up, finishing with a layer of potatoes. Pour the warm milk mixture over the top.

Bake in the preheated oven until the milk has been absorbed, about 40 minutes. Serve in the baking dish.

CODFISH BALLS

The seaports of New England, particularly in Massachusetts, grew rich on the cod trade, and dried codfish were shipped by the hundreds of thousands to Europe as early as 1623. In common with other cooks in the late eighteenth and early nineteenth centuries, Shaker Sisters used this dried fish in chowders, stews, pies and traditional codfish balls. In some Shaker recipes the fish is not soaked, which suggests either that it was not as heavily salted as that sold today or that a very salty taste was preferred.

4–6 SERVINGS

¾ pound salt cod fillets
1 pound potatoes, peeled and diced
1 egg, beaten
⅛ teaspoon grated nutmeg
pepper
oil for frying
lemon wedges for serving

Put the salt cod fillets in a bowl of cold water and let soak 12–24 hours. Change the soaking water several times. When ready, the fish should feel soft, similar to fresh cod. Drain well and flake the fish, discarding any skin.

Put the flaked fish and potatoes in a saucepan and cover with fresh cold water. Bring to a boil, then reduce the heat and simmer until the potatoes are tender, 12–15 minutes.

Drain the fish and potatoes and return them to the pan. Cover with a crumpled dish towel and set aside for a few minutes: the towel will absorb the moisture in the steam, leaving the potatoes dry.

Beat the potatoes and fish together until quite smooth. Beat in the egg, nutmeg and pepper to taste.

Heat 2–3 inches of oil in a large frying pan until it is very hot (375°F on a deep-frying thermometer). Drop the fish mixture into the hot oil in spoonfuls to make balls about the size of a small egg. Fry until puffy and golden brown, turning to color evenly. Drain the fish balls on paper towels and serve hot, with lemon wedges or crisply fried bacon.

BOILED FISH WITH A RICH SAUCE

The fish here is not actually boiled but is gently poached in a flavored liquid. In some Shaker recipes, the liquid was thickened by whisking it into 3 or more whole eggs or egg yolks, which requires skill as this sort of mixture can easily curdle.

4 SERVINGS

1 cup dry hard cider or white wine
3 cups water
1 onion, minced
1 celery stalk, minced
2 carrots, minced
1 bay leaf
a few fresh thyme sprigs
4 fish steaks, cut ¾-inch thick
2 teaspoons cornstarch mixed with 1 tablespoon cold water
1 egg yolk, lightly beaten with 2 tablespoons heavy cream
salt and pepper
3–4 tablespoons chopped fresh chives

Combine the cider or wine and water in a frying pan or other shallow pan large enough to accommodate the fish steaks. Add the minced vegetables, bay leaf and thyme sprigs. Bring to a boil, then reduce the heat and let simmer gently 20 minutes.

Put the fish into the liquid. Simmer very gently about 8 minutes or until the fish is cooked. To test make a slit with a sharp knife: the flesh next to the bone should still be slightly translucent.

Lift the fish out of the liquid onto a platter and keep warm.

Boil the cooking liquid until it has reduced to about ¾ cup. Strain it into a saucepan. Bring back to a boil, then whisk in the cornstarch mixture. Whisk until thickened. Whisk a spoonful of the thickened sauce into the egg yolk mixture, then add this to the remaining sauce in the pan. Bring just to a boil, whisking. Season with salt and pepper and stir in the chives.

Spoon the sauce over the fish steaks and serve.

COOK'S NOTE You could prepare a whole fish or piece of a large fish in the same way, allowing 25–30 minutes cooking (according to thickness).

OVERLEAF: FISH AND EGGS (LEFT), CODFISH BALLS

BAKED FISH WITH HERB DRESSING

Some Shaker recipes for baked fish used fish stock to bind the cracker meal dressing, and covered the fish with salt pork for baking.

6–8 SERVINGS

1 whole fish weighing 4–5 pounds, cleaned and
scaled if necessary
1 cup cracker crumbs
2-3 tablespoons minced fresh parsley
1 small handful of fresh dill, minced
1 small garlic clove, minced (optional)
3 tablespoons butter, melted
salt and pepper
1 egg, beaten
cornmeal
4–6 bacon slices

Preheat the oven to 350°F.

Remove the head and tail from the fish. It can then be boned or cut in two fillets. Keep all the trimmings for making a fish stock, if desired. Rinse the fish under cold running water and pat dry with paper towels.

Mix together the cracker crumbs, herbs, garlic and butter. Season with salt and pepper. Bind with the egg.

Stuff the boned fish with the herb dressing; or spread the dressing over one fish fillet and set the other fillet on top, to reshape the fish. "Sew" the opening(s) closed with metal skewers or poultry lacers (or use wooden toothpicks). Lay the fish in a buttered baking dish and dredge lightly with cornmeal. Score three or four diagonal slashes on the top side. Lay the bacon slices evenly over the fish. Pour a little water, fish stock or white wine into the dish.

Bake 35–40 minutes, basting occasionally with the liquid in the dish. To test if the fish is cooked, make a slit into the flesh with a sharp knife: the flesh should still be slightly translucent in the center. Serve hot, with lemon wedges.

FRIED CHICKEN WITH CREAM GRAVY

The method of coating chicken pieces with seasoned flour or batter and then frying them in hot fat until crisp and golden brown originated in the South, possibly introduced by the Scots who settled there. It gradually made its way northwards, where the Shaker Sisters no doubt tried it and found it delicious, particularly when paired with a gravy made from the rich cream produced in the Shaker dairies.

6 SERVINGS

2 broiler-fryer chickens, each weighing about
2½ pounds, cut in pieces
½ cup flour
½ teaspoon salt
½ teaspoon pepper
½ teaspoon paprika
½ teaspoon dried marjoram or oregano
2 tablespoons butter
3 tablespoons bacon drippings, lard or vegetable oil
1 cup light cream or ½ cup milk plus ½ cup
light cream

Rinse the chicken pieces and pat dry with paper towels. Put the flour, salt, pepper, paprika and marjoram in a plastic bag and shake to mix. Add the chicken pieces, two or three at a time, and shake to coat with the seasoned flour. Shake off excess flour and set the pieces on a rack.

Heat the butter and fat or oil in a large heavy skillet or chicken fryer over medium-high heat. When the fat is hot, put in the chicken pieces, in one layer (fry in batches if necessary). Fry until well browned, turning so the pieces color evenly.

Remove the chicken pieces and reserve. Pour excess fat from the pan. Add the cream or cream and milk mixture to the pan and stir to mix with the sediments. Return the chicken pieces. Cover and cook over a low heat until the chicken is cooked and tender, 20–25 minutes.

Transfer the chicken to a platter. Whisk the cream gravy to blend it evenly, and check the seasoning. Pour the gravy over the chicken and serve.

CHESTNUT AND HERB DRESSING FOR TURKEY

At one time, chestnut trees grew in great forests all the way from Maine to Alabama, and chestnuts were used by Shaker cooks in both sweet and savory dishes. Unfortunately, nearly all the native trees were killed by a chestnut blight in 1904, and it took over 30 years for them to recover.

MAKES ABOUT 10 CUPS

1 cup butter
3 large yellow onions, minced
3 large celery stalks with leaves, minced
about 1 cup boiling water
8 cups crumbled or cubed day-old bread
2 tablespoons minced fresh thyme
2 tablespoons minced fresh marjoram
1 tablespoon minced fresh rosemary
1½ cups chopped freshly cooked or canned chestnuts
salt and pepper
2 eggs, beaten

Melt 4 tablespoons of the butter in a heavy skillet. Add the onions and celery and cook over medium heat until the vegetables are soft but not brown. Remove from the heat and let cool slightly.

Put the remaining butter in a bowl, pour in the boiling water and stir to melt the butter. Add the bread and toss with a fork to moisten.

Add the softened vegetables to the bowl together with the herbs and chestnuts. Season with salt and pepper. Add the eggs and mix well. Let the dressing cool before stuffing the turkey.

COOK'S NOTE The dressing will stuff a turkey weighing 10–12 pounds. It can also be baked in a buttered dish, covered, in 350–375°F oven for 30–45 minutes.

CHICKEN BREASTS WITH FRIED APPLES

Visitors from the World, who came to enjoy a meal at the bountiful Shaker table, would often be served chicken, and they always remembered how yellow and rich the meat was.

4 SERVINGS

2 tablespoons butter
2 tart green apples such as Granny Smith's, cored and sliced across in rings
1 tablespoon vegetable oil
4 skinless boneless chicken breast halves
¼ cup apple cider
1 teaspoon grated lemon zest
4 tablespoons heavy cream
salt and pepper

Heat the butter in a heavy skillet over medium-low heat. Add the apple rings and turn to coat with butter. Fry until tender and very lightly browned, about 15 minutes, turning occasionally. Remove the apples with a slotted spatula and drain on paper towels. Keep warm.

Add the oil to the skillet and heat over medium-high heat. When hot, add the chicken breasts and cook until golden brown, 2–3 minutes on each side.

Add the cider and lemon zest and bring to a boil. Cover and simmer over medium heat until the chicken is cooked and tender, 5–10 minutes longer.

Remove the chicken from the pan and keep warm. Add the cream and bring the liquid back to a boil. Season with salt and pepper. Boil until reduced to a saucelike consistency, 1–2 minutes.

Pour the sauce over the chicken, garnish with the fried apple rings and serve.

CHICKEN POTPIE

The Shakers raised large flocks of chickens, and no part of the bird was ever wasted. The fat was rendered to use as a substitute for butter in chicken dishes as well as in piecrust pastries, cookies, puddings and biscuits.

6 SERVINGS

3 tablespoons butter
1 onion, minced
1 celery stalk, thinly sliced
½ pound mushrooms, quartered
3 tablespoons flour
2 cups rich chicken stock, preferably homemade
½ cup light cream
1 tablespoon minced fresh parsley
2 cups shelled fresh or thawed frozen peas
3 cups diced cooked chicken
salt and pepper

FOR THE BISCUIT DOUGH

2 cups flour
1 tablespoon baking powder
½ teaspoon salt
½ teaspoon sugar
6 tablespoons butter
1 tablespoon minced fresh rosemary
¾ cup buttermilk

Preheat the oven to 425°F.

Melt 1 tablespoon of the butter in a saucepan, add the onion, celery and mushrooms and cook over a low heat until softened. With a slotted spoon, remove the vegetables from the pan and set aside. Melt the remaining butter in the pan, stir in the flour and cook, stirring, about 2 minutes. Gradually stir in the stock and bring to a boil. Cook, stirring, until thickened. Let simmer gently 5–10 minutes.

Meanwhile, make the biscuit dough. Sift the flour, baking powder, salt and sugar into a bowl. Cut in the butter until coarse crumbs are formed. Add the rosemary. Gradually mix in the buttermilk to make a soft dough, kneading as little as possible. Roll out the biscuit dough to about ½-inch thickness.

Stir the cream and parsley into the sauce. Add the peas, chicken and softened vegetables. Season with salt and pepper. Pour the mixture into a 1½- to 2-quart baking dish or casserole that is at least 2 inches deep. Lay the rolled-out biscuit dough over the top and press onto the rim of the dish. Crimp or fork the edge if desired. Cut three or four slashes in the crust.

Bake until the biscuit crust is risen and golden brown and the filling is bubbling, 25-30 minutes. Serve hot, in the baking dish.

COOK'S NOTE The biscuit dough can be cut in 2-inch rounds, placed on a buttered baking sheet and baked at 450°F for 10–12 minutes.

PREVIOUS PAGES: CHICKEN POTPIE (LEFT), CHICKEN BREASTS WITH FRIED APPLES

HOT TURKEY OR CHICKEN AND MUSHROOM SANDWICHES

Although primarily observed as a religious day of forgiving, Christmas was joyfully celebrated in Shaker communities, and the dining room was festooned with wreaths and garlands. A feast was enjoyed at Thanksgiving, too, with roast chicken normally given pride of place. Recipes for using up the leftovers were always being devised by the Shaker Sisters.

6 SERVINGS

4 tablespoons turkey or chicken drippings or butter
1 yellow onion, minced
1 pound mushrooms, trimmed and sliced
3½ tablespoons flour
2 cups turkey or chicken stock made from the carcass
2 teaspoons minced fresh thyme
a large dash of Worcestershire sauce or more to taste
salt and pepper
¾ pound cooked turkey or chicken, cut in medium-thick slices
6 thick slices of bread, buttered if desired

Heat the drippings or butter in a wide pan, add the onion and mushrooms and cook over medium heat until the onion is soft and the mushrooms are wilted (they will exude liquid). Sprinkle over the flour and stir in well, then gradually stir in the stock. Bring to a boil, stirring. Add the thyme and Worcestershire sauce, and season with salt and pepper. Let simmer gently 10 minutes, stirring frequently.

Put the slices of turkey or chicken into the mushroom gravy (add them one at a time so they are coated on both sides) and heat through 2–3 minutes.

Divide the sliced turkey or chicken among the bread slices. Spoon the mushroom gravy over the top and serve.

MEAT LOAF

As cooks were advised on a Shaker sales leaflet, herbs "give character to food and add charm and variety to ordinary dishes." That is certainly the case with an ordinary dish such as meat loaf.

4–6 SERVINGS

1 pound lean ground beef
½ pound ground veal
½ pound ground pork
1 small onion, minced
2 tablespoons minced fresh parsley
2 teaspoons chopped fresh thyme
2 teaspoons chopped fresh sage
1 teaspoon salt or more to taste
¼ teaspoon pepper or more to taste
1 egg
¾ cup half-and-half or milk
½ tablespoon prepared mustard
½ cup cracker crumbs or bread crumbs
⅓ cup beef stock

Preheat the oven to 350°F.

Combine the meats, onion, herbs, salt and pepper in a bowl. In another bowl, lightly beat the egg with the half-and-half or milk and mustard. Add the crumbs and stir to mix. Add the crumb mixture to the meat mixture and toss together, using a fork to blend the ingredients lightly but thoroughly.

Spoon the meat mixture into the center of a shallow baking pan and shape into a long bolster shape, pressing together firmly but gently. Pour the stock around the meat loaf. Bake until browned and cooked through, about 1½ hours, basting occasionally with the juices in the pan. Let rest 5–10 minutes before cutting into slices.

COOK'S NOTE If you prefer, use 1½ pounds beef with ½ pound pork.

BEEF STEW WITH HERB DUMPLINGS

The Shakers could savor their home-raised grass-fed beef in stews such as this.

6 SERVINGS

flour
salt and pepper
2 pounds beef for stew, cut in 1½-inch cubes
1 tablespoon butter
2 tablespoons vegetable oil
4 cups hot water
8–12 small or pearl onions, peeled
4 carrots, cut in ½-inch pieces
3 celery stalks, cut in 1-inch pieces
2 turnips or parsnips, cut in ½-inch pieces
1 pound small boiling potatoes, peeled

FOR THE DUMPLINGS

¾ cup yellow cornmeal
½ cup flour
1 teaspoon baking powder
¾ teaspoon salt
3 tablespoons chopped mixed fresh herbs, eg parsley,
thyme, marjoram, lovage
1 egg, beaten
½ cup milk
1 tablespoon butter, melted

Season some flour with salt and pepper and use to coat the cubes of beef; shake off excess flour. Heat the butter with the oil in a Dutch oven or other heavy pot. When the fat is very hot, add the beef cubes and brown them on all sides. Do this in batches and keep the heat quite high. When all the beef cubes have been browned, pour in the water and bring to a boil. Reduce the heat, cover and simmer until the beef is almost tender, about 2 hours.

Add the vegetables and stir to mix. Season with salt and pepper. Bring back to a boil, then cover again and let simmer over low heat about 30 minutes.

Meanwhile, prepare the dumpling batter. Combine the cornmeal, flour, baking powder, salt and herbs in a bowl. Add the egg, milk and butter and stir to make a thick batter.

Drop the batter in 6 large spoonfuls on top of the stew. Cover and simmer until the dumplings are puffed and firm to the touch and the meat and vegetables are tender, about 15 minutes longer. Serve hot.

COOK'S NOTE Cubes of boneless venison could be substituted for the beef.

POT ROAST WITH HORSERADISH SAUCE

Shaker cooks wasted nothing – even the toughest cuts of meat from work animals would have been used in a bouillon or soup, or slowly pot roasted until tender. Beef today doesn't need the same amount of slow cooking to make it appetizing, but pot roasting still gives succulent and delicious results.

6–8 SERVINGS

2 tablespoons beef drippings or vegetable oil
1 3-pound boneless beef roast such as round or
chuck, any fat removed

1 large yellow onion, chopped
¼ cup cider vinegar
2 tablespoons cranberry catsup (page 134)
1 cup beef stock or water
3 whole cloves
salt and pepper

FOR THE SAUCE

½ cup heavy cream
1 teaspoon dry mustard
1 teaspoon sugar
¼ cup freshly grated horseradish
2 tablespoons mayonnaise
salt and pepper

Heat the drippings or oil in a Dutch oven or other pot into which the beef will just fit comfortably. When the fat is hot, put in the beef roast. Brown it well on all sides over a brisk heat, turning with two spoons. Lift out the roast and reserve.

Add the onion to the pot and stir to mix with the fat. Cook over a medium-low heat until soft and beginning to brown. Stir in the vinegar, cranberry catsup and stock or water. Add the cloves and season with salt and pepper. Bring to a boil.

Put the beef roast back in the pot. Cover and cook over a low heat until the beef is tender, 2–2½ hours.

Meanwhile, make the sauce. Mix a little cream with the mustard and sugar until smooth. Add the remaining cream and whip until thick. Stir in the horseradish and mayonnaise and season with salt and pepper. Cover and refrigerate.

Transfer the beef to a carving board and keep warm. Simmer the cooking liquid, uncovered, until reduced to about 1 cup. Strain and check the seasoning.

Slice the beef and serve with the gravy and horseradish sauce.

COOK'S NOTE If you prefer a thickened gravy, whisk in 1–2 teaspoons cornstarch mixed with 1 tablespoon cold water.

PORK CHOPS IN SOUR CREAM

Making apple cider was a traditional fall activity in Shaker communities, and the freshly pressed cider was kept in cool cellars to prevent it from fermenting too quickly.

4 SERVINGS

4 loin pork chops, weighing 7–8 ounces each, well
trimmed
dry mustard
salt and pepper
½ tablespoon butter
½ tablespoon vegetable oil
1 carrot, diced
1 celery stalk, diced
1 small onion, chopped
1 cup apple cider, or ½ cup chicken stock and
½ cup cider
½ cup thick sour cream

Season the chops on both sides with mustard, salt and pepper. Heat the butter and oil in a heavy skillet just large enough to accommodate the chops. Add the chops and brown quickly on both sides. Scatter the vegetables over and around the chops, then cover the pan and reduce the heat to low. Cook 10 minutes.

Turn the chops over. Add the cider to the pan and bring to a boil. Cover the pan again and simmer until the chops are cooked through and tender, 20–25 minutes longer. Turn the chops once or twice.

Remove the chops from the pan to a warmed serving platter and keep hot. Boil the cooking liquid, uncovered, until reduced to about ¼ cup. Strain into a saucepan, pressing well on the vegetables. Reheat the strained liquid just to boiling, then whisk in the sour cream. Season with salt and pepper. Pour the sauce over the chops and serve.

OVERLEAF: POT ROAST WITH HORSERADISH SAUCE

LAMB AND BARLEY STEW

The Shakers kept flocks of sheep both for meat and for wool. In the spring, young and tender lamb would be enjoyed; older animals provided mutton, and there are many recipes for mutton in Shaker manuscripts. This distinctively flavored meat is not easily obtainable today, but if available it can be used to make this hearty stew.

4 SERVINGS

1 tablespoon butter
1 tablespoon vegetable oil
1½ pounds boneless lamb shoulder, trimmed of excess
fat and cut in cubes
2 yellow onions, chopped
1–2 celery stalks, chopped
4–5 carrots, cut in chunks
½ cup pearl barley
2½ cups chicken stock or water
1 bay leaf
1–2 teaspoons Worcestershire sauce
salt and pepper

Heat the butter and oil in a Dutch oven or other heavy pot. Add the cubes of lamb and brown them quickly on all sides; do this in batches if necessary. Remove the lamb with a slotted spoon and set aside.

Add the vegetables to the pot, reduce the heat and fry, stirring, until the onion is soft and starting to brown. Add the barley and stir well to mix. Pour in the stock or water and add the bay leaf and Worcestershire sauce. Return the lamb cubes to the pot and season with salt and pepper. Bring to a boil, then cover and reduce the heat. Cook until the lamb and barley are tender, about 1 hour.

LAMB STEAKS WITH HERB BUTTER

The Shaker Sisters used the herbs from their garden in so many ways, both culinary and medicinal. In the kitchen, they blended dried herbs to make seasoning mixes, and mixed fresh herbs into soft butter to be used as spreads for warm bread and biscuits as well as in cooking.

4 SERVINGS

4 tablespoons soft butter
2 teaspoons minced fresh parsley
1 teaspoon minced fresh thyme
1 teaspoon minced fresh mint
1 teaspoon prepared mustard, preferably Dijon-style
a few drops of lemon juice
salt and pepper
4 lamb steaks cut from the leg

Combine the butter, herbs, mustard and lemon juice in a bowl and beat well together. Season with salt and pepper. Set aside.

Salt and pepper the lamb steaks, then cook them over charcoal, on a cast-iron ridged grill pan or under the broiler. Top each steak with a spoonful of herb butter and serve immediately.

COOK'S NOTE You can also serve the herb butter on thick lamb chops or beef steaks (omitting the mint if preferred).

LAMB SHANKS WITH DRIED FRUIT

Sauces and gravies for Shaker dishes were rarely prepared European-style, but rather were based on the juices produced in the cooking.

4 SERVINGS

4 lamb shanks, total weight 3½–4 pounds
salt and pepper
2 small yellow onions, quartered
1¾ cups chicken stock or water
½ cup plump prunes
⅓ cup plump dried apricot halves
¼ cup dried cranberries
6 whole allspice
4 whole cloves
1 bay leaf

Preheat the oven to 350°F.

Arrange the shanks in a heavy baking dish or casserole, in one layer if possible. Season the lamb shanks with salt and pepper. Tuck in the onion quarters. Add ¼ cup of the stock or water. Cover tightly and put into the oven. Cook 1 hour.

Combine the remaining ingredients, with the rest of the stock or water, in a saucepan and bring to a boil. Remove from the heat and set aside.

Add the fruit mixture to the baking dish. Cover and return to the oven. Cook until the lamb is very tender and falling from the bones and the fruit is very soft and plump, about 1 hour longer. Skim the fat from the cooking liquid before serving.

HAM BAKED IN CIDER

In American cookbooks in the late eighteenth and early nineteenth centuries there was much emphasis on pickling, and all rural homemakers produced their own brined or smoked meats. The Shakers excelled at preserving perishables, and were particulary known for their excellent smoked hams.

10 OR MORE SERVINGS

½ fully cooked ham, weighing 5–7 pounds
whole cloves
2 cups apple cider
½ cup water
2 tablespoons light brown sugar
a large strip of lemon zest

Preheat the oven to 325°F.

If there is any rind on the ham, remove it and trim off excess fat. Score the remaining surface fat in large diamond shapes, cutting through the fat and just into the flesh. Stick a clove in the center of each diamond. Set the ham in a roasting pan.

Combine the remaining ingredients in a saucepan and bring to a boil, stirring. Simmer 5 minutes.

Discard the lemon zest, then pour the mixture over the ham. Bake until the ham is hot all the way through, about 1½ hours, basting frequently with the cider mixture in the pan. (The internal temperature of the ham should be 155°F on a meat thermometer.)

Transfer the ham to a carving board and keep warm. Pour the cider mixture into a saucepan. Skim off surface fat, then bring to a boil and boil until syrupy. Brush this syrupy glaze over the ham and leave for a few minutes before carving.

COOK'S NOTE If possible, use a country ham.

OVERLEAF: LAMB STEAKS WITH HERB BUTTER (LEFT), HAM AND POTATO HASH

BACON AND EGG HAND PIES

For the Shakers, picnics were much-anticipated treats, and small savory pies usually formed part of the repast.

MAKES 4

4 thick-cut slices of country-style bacon
4 small eggs
pepper
1 egg yolk beaten with 2 teaspoons water

FOR THE PASTRY

2 cups flour
½ teaspoon salt
½ tablespoon dry mustard
½ cup vegetable shortening
½ cup grated sharp cheddar cheese or other firm well-flavored cheese
4–6 tablespoons cold water

First make the pastry. Put the flour, salt and mustard in the food processor and turn on the machine briefly to mix. Add the shortening and process until the mixture resembles crumbs, turning the machine on and off several times. Add the cheese and process briefly. Add enough water to bind the ingredients (they should still look crumbly), then turn onto the work surface and mix briefly with your hands to a smooth dough. Gather into a ball, wrap and refrigerate at least 30 minutes.

Fry the bacon until it is crisp and browned. Drain on paper towels, then crumble or chop coarsely.

Preheat the oven to 400°F.

Divide the dough into eight equal pieces. Using a saucer as a guide, roll out one piece of dough to a round that is a little larger than the saucer. Dust the saucer with flour, then line it with the round of dough. Scatter in a crumbled slice of bacon and make a little well in the center. Break an egg over the top, centering the yolk in the well. Season with pepper. Roll out a second piece of dough to make the top crust. Press the edges together to seal, then roll them over together, pressing well. (Be sure to seal well or the egg will escape.) Make one or two small slits in the top crust. Transfer the pie to a baking sheet. Make three more pies in the same way.

Brush the tops of the pies with the egg yolk glaze. Bake until golden brown and crisp, about 20 minutes. Serve hot or cold.

HAM AND POTATO HASH

4 SERVINGS

2 tablespoons butter
1–2 tablespoons vegetable oil
1 yellow onion, minced
1½ pounds boiling potatoes, peeled and diced
1½ cups minced cooked ham (about ½ pound)
2 eggs, beaten
1–2 teaspoons prepared mustard
salt and pepper

Heat 1 tablespoon each of butter and oil in a nonstick frying pan or well seasoned skillet. Add the onion and potatoes and cook until tender and lightly browned, stirring frequently.

Turn the onion and potatoes into a bowl and add the ham, eggs and mustard. Season with salt and pepper. Mix well.

Heat the remaining butter in the frying pan, with more oil if necessary. Spoon in the ham and potato mixture and spread out evenly, pressing down into a cake. Cook until browned on the base, about 5 minutes. Then turn over and brown the other side (or brown under the broiler without turning). Cut in wedges to serve.

COOK'S NOTE You could substitute leftover cooked potatoes, adding them to the onion with the ham.

CHAPTER THREE

VEGETARIAN DISHES

At a time when the World's people were eating meals that contained lots of meat, much of it salted, and drinking copious amounts of spirits, the Shakers adopted a vegetarian regime. It was not rigidly enforced in all the communities, but the kitchen Sisters devised such appetizing meatless fare that it would have been appealing to all but the most traditional of Believers.

LENTIL LOAF

4–6 SERVINGS

2 cups green lentils
¼ cup minced onion
1 garlic clove, minced (optional)
1 tablespoon chopped fresh parsley
1 tablespoon chopped fresh sage
2 teaspoons chopped fresh thyme
salt and pepper
1¼ cups shredded sharp cheddar cheese
1 cup fresh bread crumbs
¼ cup chopped walnuts
1 egg, beaten
melted butter

FOR THE TOMATO SAUCE

2 pounds ripe tomatoes, seeded and chopped
1 tablespoon butter
½–1 teaspoon sugar
3–4 tablespoons grated fresh horseradish

Vegetarianism is not yet incorporated into the Society, although beyond all doubt it is destined someday to become so. But in our Family there are quite a number of vegetarians, and I enjoy the privilege, which I dearly prize, of eating at a table bounteously spread with good nourishing food, but unpolluted with the products of the shambles in any shape or form...

FROM *SHAKER AND SHAKERESS*, NOVEMBER, 1873

Put the lentils in a saucepan, cover with cold water and bring to a boil. Reduce the heat and simmer until the lentils are very soft. Drain well and let cool.

Preheat the oven to 350°F.

Combine the lentils, onion, garlic and herbs in a bowl. Season with salt and pepper. Add 1 cup of the cheese, the crumbs and walnuts and mix well together. Mix in the egg to bind the ingredients.

Spoon the mixture onto the center of a lightly greased baking pan and mold the mixture into a flattened loaf shape, pressing firmly. Brush the loaf all over with melted butter and scatter the remaining cheese over the top.

Bake until firm and lightly browned, about 45 minutes.

Meanwhile, make the tomato sauce. Put the tomatoes and butter in a heavy saucepan and simmer until very soft and reduced, about 20 minutes. Purée in a blender or food processor, then press through a fine strainer and return to the pan. Stir in the sugar and season with salt and pepper. Add the horseradish and set aside.

Let the lentil loaf cool 5 minutes, then slice and serve with the warm tomato sauce.

VEGETABLE POTPIE

The potpie – truly an American invention – usually has a chicken, beef or pork filling. But during the time of the Shakers' "bloodless diet," only vegetables would have been used.

4–6 SERVINGS

2 tablespoons butter
1 large yellow onion, sliced
1 green apple, peeled, cored and chopped
2 tablespoons flour
1¼ cups milk
salt and pepper
2 carrots, cut in ¼-inch slices
2 celery stalks, cut in ¼-inch slices
1 cup rutabaga cut in small cubes
3 medium-size boiling potatoes, cut in small cubes
cheese pastry for a double-crust pie (page 62, Bacon and Egg Hand Pies)

Melt the butter in a saucepan, add the onion and fry until soft but not browned. Stir in the apple and cook 1 minute, then stir in the flour. Cook 1–2 minutes longer, stirring constantly. Gradually stir in the milk and bring to a boil. Simmer very gently about 5 minutes, stirring occasionally. Season with salt and pepper. Set aside.

Steam the carrots, celery, rutabaga and potatoes until just tender. Add to the onion and apple sauce. Stir to mix. Let cool slightly.

Preheat the oven to 400°F.

On a lightly floured surface, roll out two-thirds of the pastry dough thinly and use to line a shallow 1½-quart casserole. Fill with the vegetable mixture. Roll out the remaining pastry dough for the top crust and crimp the edges to seal. Cut a cross in the center of the top crust to make a steam vent hole.

Bake until the pastry is golden brown, 40–45 minutes. Serve hot.

ASPARAGUS AND CHEDDAR PUDDING

Savory bread puddings were a very popular supper dish, being both economical and filling. The recipes were often just buttered bread, lots of cheese, eggs and cream – simple but delicious.

6 SERVINGS

¾–1 pound tender asparagus spears
8 slices of bread, crusts trimmed if desired
soft butter
1 cup shredded sharp cheddar or other firm well-flavored cheese
1 teaspoon dry mustard
2 cups milk or 1 cup milk and 1 cup light cream
3 eggs
salt and pepper

Trim the tough ends from the asparagus spears, cutting the spears to fit the width of the baking dish (a 9½- × 7½-inch dish works well). Lay the asparagus spears in a wide pan of boiling salted water. Bring the water back to a boil, then simmer until the asparagus is just tender, 6–8 minutes. Lift out and drain on paper towels. Alternatively, steam the asparagus until tender.

Preheat the oven to 350°F.

Butter the slices of bread. Arrange half of them on the bottom of the baking dish, buttered side down. Trim the bread to fit if necessary. Lay the asparagus spears on top in one layer, alternating the direction the spears are pointing, and sprinkle with half of the cheese. Cover with the remaining bread slices, buttered side up, and sprinkle on the rest of the cheese.

Dissolve the mustard in 1 tablespoon milk in a bowl. Add the eggs and remaining milk and season with salt and pepper. Beat together lightly. Pour evenly over the bread in the baking dish, then press down so the top layer of bread is moistened.

Bake until puffy, golden brown and crisp on top, 30–40 minutes. Serve hot.

TOMATO CREAM PIE

When tomatoes made their appearance in American cookbooks, in the mid-nineteenth century, the instructions were to cook them for several hours to make sauces and catsups, but not to eat them raw. However, the Shakers were growing tomatoes as early as 1823, and enjoyed them raw, fried and baked in a delicious pie. They also canned great quantities of tomatoes for use throughout the winter.

6 SERVINGS

pastry for a double-crust pie (page 127, Lemon Pie, or your favorite recipe)
soft butter
1½ pounds firm, well-flavored tomatoes
1–1½ tablespoons light brown sugar or more to taste (according to the sweetness of the tomatoes)
¼ teaspoon grated nutmeg
about 1 teaspoon flour
salt and pepper
½ cup heavy cream
1 egg

Preheat the oven to 375°F.

Roll out just over half of the pastry dough and use to line a 9-inch pie plate. Rub a film of soft butter over the bottom of the piecrust.

If the tomatoes have tough skins, you may want to peel them. Slice the tomatoes. Spread out the slices on paper towels and let drain 5–10 minutes.

Layer the tomato slices in the piecrust, sprinkling each layer with brown sugar, nutmeg, flour, salt and pepper. Lightly beat the cream with the egg and pour over the tomatoes, filling the gaps between the slices.

Roll out the remaining pastry dough for the top crust and crimp the edges together to seal. Make a few small holes or slits in the top crust for steam vents.

Bake the pie until the pastry is golden brown, 35–40 minutes. Serve hot or at room temperature.

SMOTHERED ONION PIE

Even after the experiment with vegetarianism came to an end, meatless dishes remained popular on Shaker tables.

6–8 SERVINGS

4 tablespoons butter
2–3 large yellow onions, total weight about 1¼ pounds, thinly sliced
2 leeks, total weight about 1 pound, trimmed of dark green and thinly sliced
¼ cup minced fresh parsley
salt and pepper
1 cup fine bread crumbs from day-old bread
⅓ cup chopped walnuts
2 eggs
¾ cup sour cream

FOR THE PIECRUST

1¼ cups flour
¼ teaspoon salt
½ cup vegetable shortening
3–4 tablespoons cold water
soft butter

Melt 2 tablespoons of the butter in a heavy frying pan. Add the onions and leeks and cover the pan. Cook over medium-low heat until the onions and leeks are very soft and light golden in color, about 30 minutes. Stir from time to time.

While the onions and leeks are cooking, make the pastry for the piecrust. Put the flour and salt in the food processor and turn the machine on briefly to blend. Add the shortening and process until the mixture resembles coarse crumbs, turning the machine on and off several times. Add enough water to bind the ingredients (the mixture should still look crumbly). Turn onto the work surface and mix briefly with your hands to make a smooth dough. Gather into a ball, wrap and refrigerate 20 minutes.

Uncover the frying pan and cook briskly to evaporate excess liquid from the onions and leeks, stirring. Remove from the heat and stir in the parsley. Season with salt and pepper. Set aside.

Preheat the oven to 375°F.

Roll out the pastry dough and use to line a 9-inch pie plate. Brush a film of soft butter over the bottom of the piecrust.

Melt the remaining butter in a small pan. Remove from the heat and stir in the crumbs. Add the walnuts. Set aside.

Spread the onion mixture in the piecrust. Lightly beat the eggs with the sour cream and pour over the onions. Scatter the buttered crumbs and walnuts on top.

Bake until the pastry is golden brown and the filling is just set, 25–30 minutes. Serve hot or at room temperature.

OVERLEAF: BAKED STUFFED ACORN SQUASH (LEFT), LENTIL LOAF

Fluffy Cheese and Chive Omelet

In the dairies the Shaker Sisters made cheeses of all kinds from cream and milk, both whole and skim. Many were flavored with herbs.

4 SERVINGS

1 cup creamy soft cheese, e.g. fromage blanc
¼ cup chopped fresh chives, with the chive
flowers if available
salt and pepper
6 eggs, separated
a pinch of cream of tartar
1 tablespoon milk or water
2 tablespoons butter

Preheat the oven to 350°F.

Mix the cheese with the chopped chives in a bowl. Season with salt and pepper. Set the bowl in a pan of hot water and leave to warm slightly, stirring occasionally.

In a large bowl, beat the egg whites until frothy. Add the cream of tartar and continue beating until the whites will hold stiff peaks. Put the egg yolks in another bowl and beat with the milk or water and some seasoning until pale and thickened. Add a large spoonful of the whites to the egg yolks and beat in lightly, then fold in the remaining whites gently but thoroughly.

Melt the butter in a large skillet (10½–12 inches in diameter) with an ovenproof handle. Pour in the egg mixture and spread it out evenly. Cook over low heat, without stirring, until the omelet is set around the edges but still soft in the center, about 5 minutes. Lift the edge of the omelet gently with a knife to check the color of the base – it should be golden brown.

Transfer to the oven and bake until puffed up, set and lightly browned, about 5 minutes.

Make a shallow cut down the center of the omelet and spoon the cheese and herb mixture down the cut. Scatter on the chive flowers, then fold the omelet over in half. Slide onto a plate and serve.

Spinach Custard with Tomato Sauce

Vegetable-based custards were often made with rich cream and cheese from the spotlessly clean Shaker dairies and fresh eggs from the hen house.

4 SERVINGS

1½ pounds fresh spinach, stems removed
6 ounces creamy soft cheese or cottage cheese (about
¾ cup)
1 cup light cream
2 eggs
1 egg yolk
1 tablespoon chopped fresh tarragon
salt and pepper

FOR THE TOMATO SAUCE

1½ pounds ripe plum tomatoes, peeled and chopped
1 tablespoon butter
2 teaspoons tomato paste
½–1 teaspoon sugar
a few drops of Tabasco sauce (optional)

First make the tomato sauce. Put the tomatoes and butter in a heavy saucepan and simmer until very soft and reduced, about 20 minutes, stirring occasionally. Stir in the tomato paste and sugar to taste. Add Tabasco sauce if desired and season with salt and pepper. Set aside.

Preheat the oven to 325°F.

Wash the spinach leaves thoroughly. Put the damp leaves in a large pot. Cover and steam until wilted, then uncover and simmer rapidly, stirring, until all the spinach is tender. Drain in a colander. When the spinach is cool enough to handle, squeeze out excess liquid. Chop the spinach coarsely.

Combine the cream cheese or cottage cheese, cream, eggs, egg yolk and tarragon in a food processor. Work until smoothly blended. Add the spinach and season with salt and pepper. Process a few seconds to mix well.

'Shakers,' or 'Believers,' enjoy the products of nature, with which they are amply supplied, and use all the comforts and conveniences which the fruits of their industry permit. They live not in luxury, but in comfort; not in extravagance but in sufficiency...An evidence that their daily life is far from being austere, is afforded by their records of mortality, which prove a greater longevity among the Shakers than any other class of people.

FROM *THE SHAKER*, DECEMBER, 1871

Pour the spinach mixture into a lightly buttered 1-quart baking dish. Bake until set, 30–35 minutes. Just before serving, warm the tomato sauce. Serve the spinach custard hot, with the sauce.

MUSHROOM AND RICE CAKES

At a time when city dwellers ate steak and pie for breakfast and lots of greasy food, the Shakers were advocating plain, wholesome food – plenty of fruit and vegetables and whole-grain flours for bread.

4 SERVINGS

2 tablespoons butter
½ pound mushrooms, chopped
1½ cups cooked rice, white or brown
1 cup mashed potatoes
¼ cup chopped fresh parsley
½ teaspoon grated lemon zest
salt and pepper
2 eggs
flour
fine cracker crumbs or toasted bread crumbs
oil for frying

Melt the butter in a heavy skillet. Add the mushrooms and cook until they are wilted, then continue cooking until the excess liquid has evaporated. Let cool.

Combine the mushrooms, rice and potatoes in a bowl. Add the parsley and lemon zest and season with salt and pepper. Lightly beat one of the eggs and add to the bowl. Mix the ingredients together thoroughly.

With well floured hands, shape the mushroom and rice mixture into eight cakes. Lightly beat the remaining egg. Dip the floured cakes in the beaten egg, then coat with crumbs, patting them on gently. Refrigerate to set the coating, 20–30 minutes.

Heat about ½ inch of oil in a heavy skillet and fry the cakes until they are a rich golden brown and crisp on both sides. Drain on paper towels and serve hot.

COOK'S NOTE The mashed potatoes should be quite dry in texture.

ELDRESS BERTHA LINDSAY AND SISTERS GOING TO BLACKSMITH ORCHARD
TO PICK APPLES, CANTERBURY SHAKER VILLAGE

BAKED STUFFED ACORN SQUASH

Not all Shakers wanted to follow a vegetarian diet, so tables were divided to allow those following the "bloodless" diet to eat separately from those eating a "regular" diet. However, the delicious vegetarian dishes devised by the kitchen Sisters would have been appealing to both.

4 SERVINGS

4 acorn squash or other small winter squash, each
weighing 1–1¼ pounds
2 tablespoons butter
½ yellow onion, chopped
8 plump prunes, pitted and chopped
2 green apples, peeled, cored and chopped
¼ cup apple cider
¼ teaspoon ground ginger
salt and pepper
½ cup chopped butternuts or walnuts

Preheat the oven to 400°F.

Cut the squash in half and scoop out the seeds and fibers. Arrange the squash halves, cut side down, in a shallow baking pan. Pour a little water into the pan. Bake the squash until just tender when pierced with a knife, 25–30 minutes.

Meanwhile, melt the butter in a heavy saucepan, add the onion and cook until soft and golden. Stir in the prunes, apples, cider and ginger. Season with salt and pepper. Bring to a boil and simmer 2 minutes. Remove from the heat and stir in the nuts. Set aside.

Turn the squash over. Season with salt and pepper. Fill the central hollows with the apple and prune mixture, packing it down and doming the top slightly. Return to the oven and bake until the filling is hot and lightly browned, about 15 minutes. Serve hot.

FRIED CORNMEAL MUSH WITH ZUCCHINI

The cornmeal ground by the Shakers from their dry corn would have been much more nutritious than that made commercially today because it would have contained the whole grain. It would also have required more cooking to make mush, which was once a mainstay of American breakfasts.

4 SERVINGS

3 cups water
1 teaspoon salt
1 cup yellow cornmeal
1 tablespoon butter plus more for frying
1 tablespoon vegetable oil
1½–1¾ pounds zucchini, thinly sliced
1 tablespoon chopped fresh thyme
2 tablespoons chopped fresh marjoram
salt and pepper
tomato sauce (page 72, Spinach Custard), warmed

Put the water and salt in a saucepan and bring to a boil. Gradually sprinkle in the cornmeal, stirring constantly. Cook, stirring, until very thick and bubbly.

Pour the cornmeal mush into a buttered 9-inch square pan. Let cool, then refrigerate overnight to set.

The next day, cut the mush into squares or other shapes. Set aside.

Heat the butter with the oil in a heavy skillet. Add the zucchini. Cook over medium heat until just tender, 8–10 minutes, stirring occasionally. Stir in the herbs and season with salt and pepper. Remove from the heat and keep warm.

Fry the squares of cornmeal mush in hot butter until golden brown on both sides. Serve topped with the zucchini and tomato sauce.

COOK'S NOTE If using dried thyme and marjoram, add when frying the zucchini.

CHAPTER FOUR

SIDE DISHES

Both fresh and dried vegetables received simple treatment – often cooked in cream, a method that produces delicious results, as well as steamed or simmered in very little water. Shaker Sisters preferred to cook vegetables unpeeled if possible. Fresh salads, made from greens from the kitchen garden as well as those gathered from the wild, were originally dressed with a strong vinegar mixture sweetened with molasses.

CREAMED POTATOES

Cooking in cream was a very popular way of preparing vegetables. Original Shaker recipes would no doubt have used cream alone or very creamy milk.

4 SERVINGS

1 pound medium-size boiling potatoes
2 tablespoons butter
1 cup milk
½ cup heavy cream
salt and pepper

Put the unpeeled potatoes in a pan of salted water, bring to a boil and simmer 10 minutes. Drain. When the potatoes are cool enough to handle, peel them and cut in ½-inch slices.

Melt the butter in a large heavy nonstick skillet. Stir in the milk and cream and heat until bubbles appear around the edge. Season with salt and pepper. Add the potato slices to the pan, arranging them in one layer if possible. Reduce the heat so the liquid is simmering very gently, then let cook until the potatoes are very tender and have absorbed almost all the liquid, about 1 hour. Move the slices gently from time to time during the cooking so they don't stick to the pan. Serve hot.

FRIED TOMATOES

This is based on a recipe that appeared in *The Manifesto* in September, 1880. It is simple but very good.

4–6 SERVINGS

1 pound ripe but firm tomatoes
flour for coating
a little grated nutmeg
salt and pepper to taste
bacon drippings or butter for frying

Cut out the core from each tomato, then cut into ½-inch thick slices. Mix flour with nutmeg, salt and pepper on a plate. Dip the tomato slices in the seasoned flour to coat lightly.

Heat bacon drippings or butter in a heavy skillet until very hot. Add the tomato slices and fry until lightly browned on both sides. Serve hot

BAKED SQUASH

The large and immaculate kitchen gardens provided a wealth of produce, and vegetables and fruits were planted in rotation so that the growing season could be prolonged. In Shaker seed catalogues, an astonishing variety of vegetable seeds was offered, which included at least six kinds of squash.

6 SERVINGS

3 pounds butternut squash, halved
3–4 tablespoons pure maple syrup
2 tablespoons butter
⅛ teaspoon grated nutmeg
salt and pepper

Preheat the oven to 400°F.

Scoop out the seeds and fibers from the squash halves. Put the pieces, cut side down, on a lightly oiled baking sheet. Bake until soft and collapsed, about 1 hour. Let the squash cool slightly, then scrape the flesh from the skin. Put the flesh in a food processor.

Add the maple syrup, butter and nutmeg to the squash. Season with salt and pepper. Process until smooth.

Turn the squash mixture into a buttered baking dish. Reheat in a 350°F oven about 15 minutes. Serve hot.

COOK'S NOTE You can also use pumpkin or other winter squash, allowing for weight of skin and seeds, or sweet potatoes.

CUCUMBERS IN CREAM

The idea of cooking cucumber may seem odd, but as one Believer wrote in *The Manifesto*: "...The cucumber is one of the most valuable vegetables we raise...Even when they have become too old to be served as salad...it is then that the cucumber is at its best for cooking."

4–6 SERVINGS

3 cucumbers
2 tablespoons butter
½ teaspoon sugar
salt and pepper
½ cup heavy cream
1 tablespoon minced fresh dill

Peel the cucumbers, then cut them lengthwise in half. With the tip of a teaspoon, scrape out the central seeds. Cut across into ½-inch pieces.

Melt the butter in a heavy skillet. Add the cucumber pieces and sprinkle with the sugar. Season with salt and pepper. Sauté 4–5 minutes, stirring.

Add the cream and bring to a boil, stirring well. Stir in the dill and serve.

GLAZED CARROTS

Although Believers were encouraged to grow lemon trees "within doors," most lemons had to be bought from the World: this was one item the kitchen Sisters could not do without, whether to use as a seasoning or to make beverages and pie fillings.

4 SERVINGS

2 tablespoons butter
1 pound carrots (about 10), thinly sliced
¼ cup apple cider
1 tablespoon light brown sugar
1 teaspoon lemon juice
salt and pepper

Melt the butter in a wide heavy saucepan. Add the carrots and cider. Cover and cook 5 minutes, stirring occasionally.

Stir in the sugar and lemon juice. Season with salt and pepper. Cook uncovered until the liquid is almost all evaporated and the carrots are glazed and tender, stirring occasionally.

GREEN BEANS WITH BACON

When it was common practice for American cooks to boil vegetables in a lot of water for a long time, Shaker Sisters preferred steaming or cooking vegetables in very little water.

4–6 SERVINGS

6 thick-cut bacon slices
1 pound green beans, trimmed
¼ cup chicken stock or water
2 teaspoons chopped fresh marjoram
⅛ teaspoon sugar
¼ cup heavy cream
salt and pepper

Fry the bacon in a heavy skillet until crisp and browned. Remove with tongs and drain on paper towels. Pour off all but a film of bacon drippings from the pan.

Add the beans to the skillet and pour in the stock or water. Add the marjoram and sugar. Bring to a boil, then cover and cook over medium-low heat until the beans are just tender, about 5 minutes, stirring from time to time.

Uncover and stir in the cream. Season with salt and pepper. Bring back to a boil. Crumble the bacon and stir it in. Simmer 1 minute, then serve.

OVERLEAF: CLOCKWISE FROM LEFT: GREEN BEANS WITH BACON, GLAZED CARROTS, BEETS IN HONEY

POTATO CAKES WITH ROSEMARY

The humble potato was transformed in the hands of the creative Shaker Sisters, into salads, pies, pancakes, soups, stews, stuffings, hash, breads and side dishes.

6 SERVINGS

3 cups mashed potatoes
1 egg
1½ tablespoons minced fresh rosemary
salt and pepper
about 1 cup flour
butter for frying

Put the potatoes in a bowl, add the egg and beat until smoothly blended. Mix in the rosemary. Season with salt and pepper.

With floured hands, divide the potato mixture into 12 equal portions. Shape each into a cake about ½-inch thick, reflouring your hands as necessary and, finally, coating each cake lightly with flour.

Heat butter in a heavy skillet. Add the potato cakes and fry over medium heat until golden brown on both sides, pressing to flatten them slightly. Serve hot.

COOK'S NOTE You can add fried onion to the potato mixture or use other herbs.

BEETS IN HONEY

In the late eighteenth century, honey, maple sugar and molasses were the commonly used sweeteners, and the Shakers produced both honey and maple sugar for their own use and to sell to the World.

4 SERVINGS

1 pound small raw beets
1 tablespoon butter
3 tablespoons cider vinegar
about 3 tablespoons water
¼ cup honey
¼ teaspoon grated orange zest
salt and pepper

Trim and peel the beets, then cut them into thin slices. Melt the butter in a wide heavy pan and add the beets, vinegar and water. Bring to a boil, then cover and cook over a low heat until the beets are tender, stirring occasionally. Add a little more water if necessary.

Stir in the honey and orange zest and season with salt and pepper. Simmer, uncovered, to evaporate any excess liquid.

SLOW-BAKED BEANS

The Shakers made great quantities of baked beans, both to eat themselves and to sell to the World, often directly from the back of a truck, in nearby towns and cities. During a ban on pork, butter was used instead of salt pork to give richness.

8 OR MORE SERVINGS

*1 pound (2 cups) dried white beans such as navy
beans, soaked overnight
1 onion, peeled
¼ pound salt pork, cut in chunks
¼ cup light molasses
¼ cup pure maple syrup
2 tablespoons cider vinegar
1 tablespoon dry mustard
salt and pepper*

Drain the beans and put them in a saucepan. Cover with fresh cold water. Bring to a boil and boil 10 minutes, then drain. Return the beans to the pan, cover with fresh water and bring to a boil. Reduce the heat and simmer gently until the beans are very tender, 1–1½ hours. (Be sure they are thoroughly cooked at this stage because they won't soften any more once mixed with the remaining ingredients.)

Drain the beans in a colander set in a bowl; reserve the liquid.

Preheat the oven to 300°F.

Put the whole onion in the bottom of an earthenware bean pot or other deep casserole and add the beans and salt pork. Mix the remaining ingredients with 1½ cups of the reserved bean liquid and pour into the pot. Stir to mix. The beans should almost be covered with liquid, so add more of the liquid if necessary.

Cover the pot and bake the beans for 3½ hours. Stir from time to time and add a little more water if the beans seem to be drying out. Uncover and bake 30 minutes more, stirring occasionally. When done the beans should be a rich brown and the liquid thick. Discard the onion before serving.

GREEN CORN FRITTERS

When corn was eaten fresh, it was called "green," meaning immature because the most widely grown varieties of corn were dried to grind into meal or for other uses.

MAKES ABOUT 12

*4–6 ears tender green (young) corn
2 eggs, beaten
2 tablespoons butter, melted, plus more for frying
¼ cup flour
¼ teaspoon sugar
salt and pepper*

Shuck the corn. With a sharp knife, cut the kernels from the cobs. Roughly chop the kernels. Or, grate off the kernels. You need about 2 cups.

Combine the eggs, melted butter, flour and sugar in a bowl. Beat together until smooth. Add the corn and season with salt and pepper.

Melt some butter in a heavy skillet. Drop heaping spoonfuls of the corn mixture into the hot butter and flatten them slightly. Fry over medium heat until golden brown, 2–3 minutes on each side. Serve the fritters hot.

OVERLEAF: SLOW-BAKED BEANS (LEFT), STEAMED BROWN BREAD

HOMEMADE NOODLES

Homemade noodles were a popular alternative to potatoes. They were often cooked in vegetable water ("pot liquor") to give them more flavor.

4 SERVINGS

2 cups flour
½ teaspoon salt
2 tablespoons soft butter
2 egg yolks
about ⅓ cup water
a little cornmeal for coating

TO FINISH

butter
chopped fresh chives

Sift the flour and salt into a bowl. Make a well in the center and put in the butter, egg yolks and water. With your fingertips, mix together the butter, yolks and water, then gradually mix in the flour. Knead to make a smooth, firm dough. Add more water if necessary.

Divide the dough into three or four portions. On a lightly floured surface, roll out each piece of dough as thinly as possible. Hang the sheets of dough over the back of a chair or over a clean broom handle and let dry 15–20 minutes.

Roll up each sheet of dough loosely, like a jelly roll, and cut across in ¾-inch slices. Unroll these noodles and toss them with a little cornmeal.

Bring a large pot of salted water to a boil. Drop in the noodles. Bring the water back to a boil and cook until the noodles are just tender, about 5 minutes (bite one to check). Drain and return to the pot. Add butter and chives and toss to coat the noodles. Serve immediately.

CABBAGE SALAD

There are many recipes for cabbage salad, or cole slaw, in Shaker manuscripts, as well as for cooking cabbage in cream and braising it with apples. Cabbage was also the essential accompaniment for corned beef.

8 SERVINGS

1 medium-size head of cabbage
1 large carrot, shredded
1 green apple, cored and grated
1–2 teaspoons caraway seeds

FOR THE BOILED DRESSING

1 teaspoon dry mustard
⅓ cup sugar
1 tablespoon flour
½ teaspoon salt
½ cup cider vinegar
2 eggs
½ cup water
2 tablespoons butter
2–4 tablespoons sour cream or plain yogurt

First make the dressing. Combine the mustard, sugar, flour, salt and vinegar in a small bowl and whisk to mix. Put the eggs and water in the top of a double boiler and whisk together. Whisk in the mustard mixture. Set over simmering water and cook until the dressing thickens, about 10 minutes, stirring frequently. Remove from the heat and stir in the butter. Let cool, then stir in the sour cream or yogurt.

Cut the cabbage into quarters and cut out the core. Slice across the quarters into fine shreds.

Combine the cabbage, carrot, apple and dressing in a large bowl. Toss well together. Add the caraway seeds and mix again. Cover and refrigerate until ready to serve.

COOK'S NOTE The boiled dressing can also be used to dress potato or other vegetable salads.

STRING BEAN SALAD

We might view the nasturtium flowers as a pretty decoration for this salad, but the Shakers' principles of thriftiness and plainness meant the flowers would not have been grown just to be admired. The original recipe added nasturtium pods too, which the Shakers also pickled.

4–6 SERVINGS

³/₄ pound string beans or other green beans
1 large bunch of scallions, thinly sliced
¹/₄ head Iceberg lettuce, shredded
2 teaspoons chopped fresh summer savory or thyme
a handful of nasturtium leaves, shredded if large
a handful of nasturtium flowers

FOR THE DRESSING

5 tablespoons salad oil
2 tablespoons lemon juice
¹/₂ teaspoon prepared mustard, preferably Dijon-style
salt and pepper

Drop the beans into a saucepan of boiling salted water and cook until just tender but still with a crunch. Drain and refresh under cold running water. Pat the beans dry with paper towels and put into a bowl.

Put the dressing ingredients in a small bowl and whisk together (or shake them together in a jar). Pour the dressing over the warm beans and toss together. Let the beans cool completely.

Just before serving, add the scallions, lettuce, savory and nasturtium leaves. Toss well. Scatter the nasturtium flowers on top and serve immediately.

CUCUMBER AND MINT SALAD

Shaker Sisters always used herbs liberally in cooking. The freshness of mint could enliven a dish of vegetables, a salad or a beverage, or flavor a sauce or pudding.

4–6 SERVINGS

1 hothouse cucumber or 2 ordinary cucumbers
a handful of fresh mint leaves
¹/₂ tablespoon sugar
3 tablespoons cider vinegar
¹/₂ cup sour cream
salt and pepper
3–4 scallions, white part only, thinly sliced

If the cucumbers are waxed, peel them. Unwaxed cucumbers do not need to be peeled, but peel them if you prefer. Cut hothouse cucumbers across into thin slices; halve ordinary cucumbers lengthwise, scrape out the seeds and then slice.

Reserve 3 or 4 mint leaves; put the rest in a large bowl. Add the sugar to the bowl. Press and mash the mint leaves with a spoon to release the oils into the sugar. Add the vinegar and stir to dissolve the sugar. Remove the mint leaves, pressing and squeezing them to extract all the liquid, and discard.

Add the sour cream to the bowl and stir to mix with the mint vinegar. Season with salt and pepper. Add the cucumber slices and scallions and toss to coat with the dressing. Cover and chill about 45 minutes.

Before serving, shred the reserved mint leaves and scatter them over the salad.

OVERLEAF: STRING BEAN SALAD (LEFT), CUCUMBER AND MINT SALAD

CHAPTER FIVE

BREADS AND BAKING

In Shaker diaries and recipe collections there are many hints and tips for making breads, biscuits and muffins. The kitchen Sisters had to bake enough to provide a variety of breads at every meal for their Families of 50 or more people. Their revolving ovens could bake dozens of loaves at a time. Cakes were treats at Sunday supper.

MAPLE WHEATEN BREAD

Shakers were among the first to advocate the use of whole grain flour in baking.

MAKES 2 LOAVES

1 package active dry yeast
1 cup warm water (105–110°F)
3 tablespoons pure maple syrup, warmed
about 1½ cups white flour
½ tablespoon salt
4 cups whole wheat flour
1 cup warm milk
2 tablespoons butter, melted and cooled, plus extra for glazing

Put the yeast, ¼ cup warm water and ½ tablespoon of the maple syrup in a small bowl. Let soak 1 minute, then whisk with a fork to dissolve the yeast.

Sift the white flour and salt into a large bowl. Add the whole wheat flour and stir to mix. Make a well in the center and pour in the yeast mixture, milk, butter and remaining maple syrup and water. Mix the ingredients in the well, then gradually draw in the flour. Continue mixing to make a soft but not sticky dough, adding more white flour if the dough feels too soft and wet or a little more liquid if the dough will not come together.

Turn the dough onto a floured surface and knead until smooth and elastic, about 10 minutes. Shape the dough into a ball. Put it in a lightly buttered bowl and rotate so that the surface of the ball is greased all over. Cover and let rise in a warm, draft-free place (about 80°F) until doubled in bulk, about 1½ hours.

Gently punch the dough to deflate it, and fold the sides to the center. Knead again for 2–3 minutes. Divide the dough in half and shape into loaves, tucking the ends under. Put into two greased 8½- or 9-inch loaf pans. Let rise in a warm place 30–45 minutes.

Preheat the oven to 400°F. Brush the loaves with melted butter, then bake until well risen and browned, 45–50 minutes. Tip the loaves out of their pans and tap the base with your knuckles: the bread should sound hollow, like a drum. Transfer to a wire rack to cool.

Wheat should be used in whole, and ground coarse...No flour should be ground so fine that the teeth have no office left them to perform...Indigestion would be as rare in America as it is in Ireland, with its potato; Scotland, with its oatmeal; Germany, with its cabbage, or in England with its good, strong common sense...beginning with the Queen, who, during some part of her reign, prohibited absolutely the whole royal household from using a single loaf of bread made from superfine ground and bolted wheat flour.

FROM *SHAKER AND SHAKERESS*, NOVEMBER, 1873

SWEET POTATO BREAD

Bread ovens in Shaker kitchens could accommodate dozens of loaf pans at a time, and the range of recipes used by the Sisters insured that those loaves provided a wonderful variety.

MAKES 1 LARGE ROUND LOAF

1 package active dry yeast
³/₄ cup warm water (105–110°F)
3 tablespoons flower blossom honey
about 6 cups flour
¹/₂ tablespoon salt
¹/₂ tablespoon grated orange zest
1 cup mashed or puréed sweet potato
³/₄ cup warm milk
2 tablespoons butter, melted and cooled
beaten egg to glaze

Put the yeast, ¹/₄ cup warm water and ¹/₂ tablespoon of the honey in a small bowl. Let soak 1 minute, then whisk with a fork to dissolve the yeast.

Sift the flour and salt into a large bowl. Add the orange zest and stir to mix. Make a well in the center and add the yeast mixture, sweet potato, milk, butter and remaining honey and water. Mix the ingredients in the well, then gradually draw in the flour. Continue mixing to make a soft but not sticky dough, adding more flour if the dough feels too soft and wet or a little more liquid if the dough will not come together.

Turn the dough onto a floured surface and knead until smooth and elastic, about 10 minutes. Shape the dough into a ball. Put it in a lightly buttered bowl and rotate so that the surface of the ball is greased all over. Cover and let rise in a warm, draft-free place (about 80°F) until doubled in bulk, 1–1¹/₂ hours.

Gently punch the dough to deflate it, and fold the sides to the center. Knead again for 2–3 minutes. Shape the dough into a large round loaf and set it on a lightly

greased baking sheet. Let rise in a warm place 30–45 minutes.

Preheat the oven to 400°F. Brush the loaf with beaten egg, then bake until well risen and browned, 45–50 minutes. Transfer to a wire rack to cool.

COOK'S NOTE You can also divide the dough and bake in loaf pans or cut into three, shape into ropes and braid.

SCENTED LEAF ROLLS

Rolls and biscuits appeared on the table for 12 o'clock dinner, to accompany meat and vegetables.

MAKES ABOUT 3¹/₂ DOZEN

1 package active dry yeast
1 cup warm water (105–110°F)
1¹/₂ tablespoons sugar
about 5¹/₂ cups flour
¹/₂ tablespoon salt
1¹/₂ cups warm milk
4 tablespoons butter, melted and cooled, plus extra for
dipping
fresh herb leaves such as lemon balm, marjoram,
thyme or lovage, washed and dried

Put the yeast, ¹/₄ cup warm water and ¹/₂ tablespoon of the sugar in a small bowl. Let soak 1 minute, then whisk with a fork to dissolve the yeast.

Sift the flour, salt and remaining sugar into a large bowl. Make a well in the center and add the yeast mixture, milk, butter and remaining water. Mix the ingredients in the well, then gradually draw in the flour. Continue mixing to make a soft but not sticky dough, adding more flour if the dough feels too soft and wet or a little more liquid if the dough will not come together.

Turn the dough onto a floured surface and knead until smooth and elastic, about 10 minutes. Shape the dough

OVERLEAF: SCENTED LEAF ROLLS (LEFT), MAPLE WHEATEN BREAD

into a ball. Put it in a lightly buttered bowl and rotate so that the surface of the ball is greased all over. Cover and let rise in a warm, draft-free place (about 80°F) until doubled in bulk, 1–1½ hours.

Gently punch the dough to deflate it, and fold the sides to the center. Knead again for 2–3 minutes. Pull off pieces of dough to make balls about 2 inches in diameter. Make a hole into the center of each ball with your finger, press in a single herb leaf or a few small ones and bring the dough around to seal. Roll into a neat ball again and smooth with your thumbs, working from the top to the base and tucking the ends under. Dip the balls in melted butter, then arrange in one or more baking pans; the balls should just touch each other. Let rise in a warm place 30–45 minutes.

Preheat the oven to 400°F. Bake the rolls until well risen and golden brown, 20–25 minutes. Transfer to a wire rack to cool. Best served warm.

COOK'S NOTE If you prefer, use some of this all-purpose white bread dough to bake loaves (egg yolk glaze the tops): 9- × 5-inch pans, 25–30 minutes at 400°F.

> That bread is eaten at all tables in connection with other food, and the benefits resulting therefrom, are easily seen. It necessitates slow eating and thorough mastication, and would be a most excellent thing for Americans, who are in the habit of bolting their food in five or ten minutes, and then run to the doctor to complain of indigestion, or to the druggist for some pills. It would be much better if they would stay at the table at least half an hour, and attend to their digestion themselves, by eating proper things in a proper manner. This would also give the doctors and druggists an opportunity of earning their livelihood by some kind of honest work.
>
> FROM *SHAKER AND SHAKERESS*, NOVEMBER, 1873

HERB AND CHEESE BREAD

The Shaker Sisters made buttermilk, cream of all kinds, cheeses and butter and used these dairy products generously in their cooking. An extract from a journal dated November 30, 1843, quoted in *Gleanings from Old Shaker Journals*, compiled by Clara Endicott Sears, reads: "We weigh our cheese. Have made twenty-nine hundred pounds."

MAKES 1 LOAF

1½ cups all-purpose flour
2 teaspoons baking powder
½ teaspoon baking soda
½ teaspoon salt
½ cup graham or whole wheat flour
1 cup grated sharp cheddar cheese or other firm
well-flavored cheese
½ tablespoon crumbled dried sage
1 teaspoon dried dill
about 1 cup buttermilk

Preheat the oven to 350°F.

Sift the all-purpose flour, baking powder, soda and salt into a bowl. Add the graham or whole wheat flour, ¾ cup of the cheese and the herbs and stir to mix. Add enough buttermilk to mix to a soft dough.

Form the dough gently into a bolster shape and put it in a buttered 8½- × 4½-inch loaf pan. Sprinkle the remaining cheese over the top.

Bake until golden brown and a skewer inserted in the center comes out clean, 50–60 minutes. Let cool in the pan for a few minutes before unmolding. Serve warm or cold.

COOK'S NOTE As an alternative to buttermilk you can use milk soured with ½ tablespoon cream of tartar.

CORN BREAD

The original varieties of corn were far less sweet than those we enjoy today, and were most often dried for storage, later to be ground into cornmeal or hominy as well as to provide cattle feed and dried cobs to burn as fuel. In early Shaker days, hundreds of pounds of corn were dried every year to sustain communities through the winter, and they perfected a means of drying corn that would keep it year round without any spoilage.

6–8 SERVINGS

1 cup yellow cornmeal
1 cup flour
1 tablespoon baking powder
³⁄₄ teaspoon salt
1 tablespoon sugar
2 eggs, beaten
1 cup milk
6 tablespoons butter
1 cup fresh corn kernels cut from the cob

Preheat the oven to 400°F.

Sift the cornmeal, flour, baking powder, salt and sugar into a bowl. Add the eggs and milk and mix to a smooth batter.

Put the butter in a 9- or 10-inch cast iron skillet or other pan with an ovenproof handle. Heat in the oven until the butter has melted. Tilt and rotate the skillet to coat with butter, then pour the remaining butter into the batter. Add the corn and mix well.

Pour the corn batter into the hot skillet and return to the oven. Bake until set and golden brown, 25–30 minutes.

Serve hot, cut in wedges.

COOK'S NOTE The batter can also be baked in a 9-inch round or square pan or in muffin tins or corn stick pans.

STEAMED BROWN BREAD

A traditional New England bread, often served with baked beans, this was still being sold by Shakers in New Hampshire in the 1930s.

MAKES 1 LOAF

¹⁄₂ cup rye flour
¹⁄₂ cup whole wheat flour
¹⁄₂ cup yellow cornmeal
¹⁄₂ teaspoon salt
1 teaspoon baking soda
1 cup buttermilk
¹⁄₃ cup light molasses
¹⁄₂ cup raisins

Thoroughly wash and dry a 1-pound coffee can (1-quart capacity). Butter it generously. Set a rack in the bottom of a kettle or other pot that is deep enough to accommodate the can, and add enough water to the kettle to cover the rack. Bring to a boil.

Combine the rye flour, whole wheat flour, cornmeal, salt and soda in a bowl. In another bowl, stir the buttermilk with the molasses until evenly blended. Add to the dry ingredients and mix well. Stir in the raisins.

Pour the batter into the can. Cover the top tightly with foil and tie on with string. Set the can on the rack in the kettle. Pour more boiling water into the kettle so that the level is halfway up the can. Reduce the heat so the water is barely simmering, then cover the kettle tightly and steam about 2 hours. Replenish the boiling water as necessary. To test if the bread is cooked, insert a long wooden skewer in the center: it should come out clean.

Remove the can from the kettle and let cool about 5 minutes, then unmold the bread onto a wire rack. Serve warm or cold.

ROSEWATER SPONGE CAKE

Flavoring extracts as we know them today were not readily obtainable, so most cooks used rosewater or citrus zest for flavoring cakes, pies and puddings. Many distilled their own rosewater – particularly so the Shakers, who made very large quantities both to use and to sell.

8 SERVINGS

4 eggs, separated
a pinch of cream of tartar
³⁄₄ cup superfine sugar
1 tablespoon rosewater
³⁄₄ cup cake flour
confectioners' sugar to sprinkle

Preheat the oven to 350°F. Butter and flour a 9-inch round cake pan and line the bottom with a disk of wax paper.

In a large bowl beat the egg whites until frothy. Add the cream of tartar and continue beating until the whites will form soft peaks. Sprinkle in 2 tablespoons of the sugar and beat until the whites will form stiff peaks. Set aside.

In another bowl, beat the egg yolks until frothy. Add the remaining sugar and continue beating until the mixture is very thick and pale – if you lift out the beaters the mixture should trail back onto the surface in a ribbon that holds its shape. Add the rosewater.

Sift the flour over the surface of the egg yolk mixture and fold it in gently but thoroughly. Add a large spoonful of the egg whites and mix in, then fold in the remainder. Pour the batter into the prepared pan. Bake until risen and lightly browned, 35–40 minutes. Let cool in the pan.

Unmold the cake. Dust the top with a little confectioners' sugar before serving. Best eaten the day of baking.

WHIPPED CREAM BISCUITS

These wonderful light-textured biscuits would have been usual fare on breakfast and supper tables.

MAKES 14–16

2 cups flour
1 tablespoon baking powder
½ teaspoon salt
a pinch of sugar
1¼ cups heavy cream
melted butter

Preheat the oven to 425°F.

Sift the flour, baking powder, salt and sugar into a bowl. In another bowl, whip the cream until it is thick but not stiff. Add to the dry ingredients and mix together thoroughly but lightly to make a soft dough.

Turn the dough onto a lightly floured surface and pat or roll out to ½-inch thickness. Use a floured 2- or 2½-inch cutter to cut out rounds (cut cleanly and don't twist the cutter). Arrange them on an ungreased baking sheet and brush the tops with melted butter.

Bake the biscuits until they are risen and golden brown, about 15 minutes. Serve hot from the oven.

PREVIOUS PAGES: WHIPPED CREAM BISCUITS (LEFT), HERB AND CHEESE BREAD

MOTHER ANN'S BIRTHDAY CAKE

The birthday of the founder of the Shaker society was Februrary 29, but it was usually celebrated March 1 unless it was a leap year. The original recipe instructions were to beat the cake batter with a handful of bruised peach twigs, "...which are filled with sap at this season of the year...This will impart a delicate peach flavor to the cake."

MAKES A 2-LAYER CAKE

6 egg whites
a pinch of cream of tartar
1½ cups sugar
1 cup soft butter
1 teaspoon pure vanilla extract
2½ cups cake flour
1 tablespoon baking powder
¾ cup milk
¾ cup peach preserves

FOR THE FROSTING

3 cups confectioners' sugar, sifted
9 tablespoons soft butter
½ tablespoon pure vanilla extract
about 2 tablespoons half-and-half or milk

Preheat the oven to 350°F. Butter and flour two 8- or 8½-inch round cake pans and line the bottom of each with a disk of wax paper.

Beat the egg whites until frothy. Add the cream of tartar and continue beating until soft peaks will form. Gradually sprinkle ¼ cup of the sugar over the whites and beat until glossy and stiff peaks will form. Set aside.

In another bowl beat the butter with the remaining sugar and the vanilla until pale and very fluffy (the consistency of whipped cream). Sift together the flour and baking powder. Gradually add to the butter mixture alternately with the milk. Add a large spoonful of the egg whites and mix in to loosen the mixture, then fold in the remaining whites with a rubber spatula.

Divide the batter equally between the prepared pans. Bake until golden brown and a wooden skewer inserted in the center comes out clean, about 30 minutes. Let cool.

When the cake layers are cold, spread one with the peach preserves and set the second layer on top.

To make the frosting, gradually beat the sugar into the soft butter to make a pale, fluffy mixture. Beat in the vanilla and enough milk to make a spreadable consistency. Spread the frosting over the top and side of the cake.

GINGERBREAD

Sometimes maple sap was boiled to a concentrated dark brown syrup that resembled molasses, and this was then used to sweeten gingerbread and baked beans in place of molasses.

MAKES A 9-INCH SQUARE CAKE

2½ cups flour
½ tablespoon baking soda
¼ teaspoon salt
2 teaspoons ground ginger
1 teaspoon ground cinnamon
¼ teaspoon ground cloves
¼ cup vegetable shortening
4 tablespoons soft butter
½ cup packed dark brown sugar
¾ cup light molasses
2 eggs
1 cup hot water

Preheat the oven to 350°F. Butter a 9-inch square pan and line the bottom with wax paper.

Sift the flour, soda, salt and spices into a bowl. Set aside.

In another bowl, cream the shortening with the butter. Add the sugar and beat until well blended and creamy. Beat in the molasses and then the eggs. Gradually add the flour mixture alternately with the water, beating well after each addition.

Pour the batter into the prepared pan. Bake until firm and a wooden skewer inserted in the center comes out clean, 35–40 minutes. Set the pan on a wire rack to cool. Serve warm or cold.

SPICY APPLESAUCE CAKE

Shaker applesauce was much loved both by the Believers and by those in the World who bought it. It was made in quantity and put up in wooden firkins or glass jars, to be ready for use in spicy cakes such as this one.

MAKES A 9-INCH SQUARE CAKE

2 cups flour
1 teaspoon baking powder
½ teaspoon baking soda
½ teaspoon salt
1 cup packed light brown sugar
½ cup granulated sugar
1 teaspoon ground cinnamon
½ teaspoon ground allspice
½ teaspoon grated nutmeg
¼ teaspoon ground cloves
½ cup soft butter
2 eggs, lightly beaten
½ cup milk
1½ cups applesauce (page 139)

Preheat the oven to 350°F. Grease and flour a 9-inch square pan. Line the bottom with wax paper.

Sift the flour, baking powder, soda, salt, sugars and spices into a bowl. Add the butter and beat to mix. Beat in the eggs and milk until the batter is evenly blended. Mix in the applesauce, keeping the pieces of apple whole.

Pour the batter into the prepared pan and spread out evenly. Bake until firm and a wooden skewer inserted in the center comes out clean, 40–45 minutes.

Serve warm or at room temperature, plain or topped with whipped cream.

COMB HONEY CAKE

The Shakers kept beehives and honey was much used as a sweetener in place of sugar. Natural raw honey has much more flavor than the purified store-bought product, as well as a positively heady aroma.

MAKES AN 8-INCH SQUARE CAKE

2½ cups flour
1 teaspoon baking powder
½ teaspoon baking soda
¼ teaspoon salt
½ teaspoon ground cinnamon
¼ teaspoon grated nutmeg
1¼ cups liquid honey from the comb plus
extra for drizzling
¾ cup butter
3 eggs, lightly beaten
¼ cup milk
¼ cup sliced almonds

Preheat the oven to 325°F. Butter and flour an 8-inch square pan and line the bottom with wax paper.

Sift the flour, baking powder, soda, salt and spices into a bowl. Set aside.

Warm the honey with the butter just until the butter has melted. Remove from the heat and beat in the eggs and milk. Gradually add to the dry ingredients, beating well after each addition.

Pour into the prepared pan and scatter the almonds over the surface. Bake until browned and a wooden skewer inserted in the center comes out clean, 1–1¼ hours. Cover with foil if the cake is browning too much.

Remove the cake from the oven and prick the surface all over with a skewer or fork. Drizzle honey evenly over the surface to glaze. Let cool in the pan set on a wire rack.

FRUIT AND NUT LOAF

Fruits from Shaker orchards, particularly apples, were dried for winter storage, and then used in breads, pies, puddings and dressing for poultry.

MAKES AN 8½-INCH LOAF CAKE

½ cup chopped dried peaches or apricots
½ cup chopped dried apples
½ cup raisins
1 cup packed light brown sugar
2 tablespoons butter
1 cup apple cider
2 cups flour
2 teaspoons baking powder
¼ teaspoon salt
1 teaspoon grated orange zest
2 eggs, lightly beaten
¾ cup chopped butternuts, walnuts or pecans

Combine the peaches, apples and raisins in a small saucepan with the sugar, butter and cider. Bring to a boil, stirring to dissolve the sugar, then remove from the heat and let cool.

Preheat the oven to 350°F. Butter and flour an 8½-inch loaf pan and line the bottom with wax paper.

Sift the flour, baking powder and salt into a bowl. Add the fruit and cider mixture, orange zest, eggs and nuts and mix together quickly and evenly.

Pour into the prepared pan. Bake until risen and golden brown and a wooden skewer inserted in the center comes out clean, about 1 hour. Cover the top with foil if it is browning too much. Let cool in the pan.

OVERLEAF: PECAN MUFFINS (LEFT), COMB HONEY CAKE

PECAN MUFFINS

Nut trees abounded in Shaker orchards – walnut, butter-nut and hickory. The delicious nut of the hickory, the pecan, takes its name from Native American languages.

MAKES 12–18 (ACCORDING TO THE PANS USED)

2 cups flour
2 teaspoons baking powder
½ teaspoon salt
½ cup packed light brown sugar
1 teaspoon ground cinnamon
½ teaspoon grated lemon zest
1 cup milk
2 eggs
4 tablespoons butter, melted and cooled
½ cup chopped pecans

Preheat the oven to 400°F.

Sift the flour, baking powder, salt, sugar and cinnamon into a bowl. Stir in the lemon zest. Combine the milk, eggs and butter and mix well. Add to the dry ingredients together with the pecans. Stir just until blended, leaving lumps in the dough.

Spoon into buttered muffin pans, filling them two-thirds full. Bake until risen and golden brown, 20–25 minutes. Let cool in the pans about 1 minute, then unmold onto a wire rack.

SUGAR COOKIES

Before the sugar tariffs were lifted, in the 1880s, white sugar was expensive, so frugal cooks used molasses, honey and maple sugar or syrup instead. With their beehives and acres of maple trees, the Shakers could be self-sufficient in these sweeteners.

MAKES ABOUT 2½ DOZEN

¾ cup soft butter
1 cup granulated maple or white sugar plus extra for sprinkling
1 teaspoon grated lemon zest
2 eggs
about 3 cups flour
½ teaspoon salt
¼ teaspoon grated nutmeg

Beat the butter with the sugar and lemon zest until well blended and creamy. Beat in the eggs. Sift the flour with the salt and nutmeg and gradually beat into the butter mixture. Add more flour if necessary to make a dough that can be rolled out. Gather into a ball, wrap and chill about 20 minutes.

Preheat the oven to 375°F.

Roll out the dough to about ½-inch thickness. Cut into rounds or other shapes with cookie cutters. Place on lightly greased baking sheets and sprinkle the cookies lightly with sugar. Alternatively, take large walnut-size pieces of dough and shape into balls. Arrange on the baking sheets, leaving plenty of space between each ball. Butter the base of a large glass, dip it in sugar and use to flatten the balls (one greasing will do, but dip the glass in sugar each time).

Bake until the cookies are lightly golden brown around the edge and just firm to the touch, about 10 minutes. Cool on a wire rack.

CINNAMON SOUR CREAM COOKIES

MAKES ABOUT 3 ¹/₂ DOZEN

¹/₂ cup soft butter
1 cup packed light brown sugar
1 egg
¹/₂ cup sour cream
¹/₂ teaspoon baking soda
2¹/₂ cups flour
1 teaspoon baking powder
¹/₄ teaspoon salt
¹/₂ tablespoon ground cinnamon

Beat the butter with the sugar until well blended and creamy. Beat in the egg. Mix together the sour cream and baking soda and add to the butter mixture. Sift the flour, baking powder, salt and cinnamon into a bowl, then add to the butter mixture. Beat well to make a soft dough. It will be sticky, so cover and chill about 30 minutes (if the kitchen is hot, you may need to chill the dough a little longer).

Preheat the oven to 375°F.

Take large walnut-size pieces of dough and roll into balls. Arrange on lightly greased baking sheets, leaving space for spreading. Flatten the balls with a floured fork. Bake until golden brown and still slightly soft in the center, 10–15 minutes.

Let cool 1–2 minutes on the baking sheets, then transfer to wire racks to cool completely.

PECAN BALLS

MAKES 2¹/₂–3 DOZEN

2 cups flour
¹/₂ teaspoon salt
1 cup soft butter
¹/₂ cup confectioners' sugar, sifted, plus extra for dusting
1 teaspoon pure vanilla extract
1 cup finely chopped pecans

Preheat the oven to 350°F.

Sift the flour with the salt and set aside. Beat the butter with the sugar and vanilla until well blended and creamy. Gradually beat in the flour, then mix in the pecans.

Take pieces of dough and roll into large walnut-size balls. Arrange on ungreased baking sheets. Bake until set and very lightly browned, 15–20 minutes.

Let cool 1 minute on the baking sheets, then transfer to wire racks. While still warm, dust with confectioners' sugar. Store in an airtight tin with more confectioners' sugar.

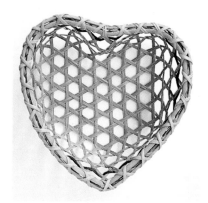

OVERLEAF: SUGAR COOKIES (LEFT), CRANBERRY OATMEAL COOKIES

A MODERN VERSION OF A SHAKER KITCHEN, SHOWING THE FAMILIAR HEART-SHAPED IMPLEMENTS
HANGING FROM THE WALL

MOLASSES COOKIES

Molasses, which is what remains after sugar cane juice is boiled until it crystallizes, was the most widely used sweetener in America in the nineteenth century. In addition to sweetening cookies, cakes, pie fillings, quick breads and so on, it was added to meat dishes and to hot and cold drinks. Shaker switchel, or "haying water," was a refreshing cold drink made from water, ginger, sugar or maple syrup, and molasses.

MAKES ABOUT 3 DOZEN

½ cup soft butter
½ cup sugar
½ cup light or dark molasses
1 egg
2 cups flour
2 teaspoons baking soda
¼ teaspoon salt
1 teaspoon ground ginger
½ teaspoon grated nutmeg
¼ teaspoon ground cloves

Preheat the oven to 375°F.

Beat the butter with the sugar and molasses until well blended and creamy. Beat in the egg. Sift the flour, soda, salt and spices into another bowl. Gradually add to the molasses mixture, beating well after each addition.

Drop heaped tablespoons of the cookie dough onto lightly greased baking sheets, leaving space for spreading. Bake until just firm in the center, 10–12 minutes. Let cool on the sheets for a few seconds, then transfer to wire racks to cool completely.

CRANBERRY OATMEAL COOKIES

Cranberry vines were cultivated on Shaker farms, and the berries were used fresh or they were canned or dried. When dried, they often replaced the more expensive raisins in baked goods and puddings.

MAKES ABOUT 2 DOZEN

¾ cup flour
½ teaspoon baking soda
½ teaspoon salt
½ teaspoon ground cinnamon
½ cup soft butter
½ cup packed light brown sugar
¼ cup granulated sugar
1 egg
½ teaspoon pure vanilla extract
1 cup rolled oats
½ cup dried cranberries

Preheat the oven to 350°F.

Sift the flour, soda, salt and cinnamon into a bowl. Set aside. In another bowl, beat the butter with the sugars until well blended and creamy. Add the egg and vanilla and beat well. Beat in the sifted dry ingredients until smooth. Stir in the oats and cranberries.

Drop heaped tablespoonfuls of cookie dough onto lightly greased baking sheets, leaving room for spreading. Flatten each cookie slightly. Bake until lightly browned, about 15 minutes. Let cool on the baking sheets about 1 minute, then transfer to a wire rack to cool completely.

CHAPTER SIX

DESSERTS, PIES AND CANDIES

At one time, pies were served at all meals, but as the nineteenth century ended it became more common to have them just at dinner and supper. Apple pie was a favorite, traditionally flavored with rosewater, and was often eaten with cheese. Simple puddings, often based on rich milk or cream, were eaten at dinner too, while candies were occasional pleasures.

APPLE AND BLACKBERRY BATTER PUDDING

Seasonal fruits, rich cream and eggs, and freshly ground spices were used to make simple desserts. The kitchen Sisters labored to produce meals for their Families that would satisfy both the body's hunger and the spirit – in keeping with the Shaker mission to "create a heaven on earth."

6–8 SERVINGS

4 green apples, peeled, cored and chopped
½ cup packed light brown sugar
½ teaspoon ground cinnamon
¼ teaspoon ground cloves
¼ teaspoon grated nutmeg
1 pint blackberries
2 eggs
½ cup granulated sugar
½ cup flour
¾ cup heavy or light cream
1 teaspoon pure vanilla extract

Preheat the oven to 350°F.

Combine the apples, brown sugar and spices and toss to mix. Put into a buttered shallow 1½-quart baking dish and scatter the blackberries evenly on top.

In a bowl, lightly whisk the eggs with the granulated sugar until the sugar has dissolved. Add the flour and mix well, then stir in the cream and vanilla until smooth. Pour this batter evenly over the fruit.

Bake until the apples are tender and the top of the pudding is set and golden brown, about 40 minutes. Serve warm.

COOK'S NOTE This pudding could also be made with plums and apricots.

BAKED RICE PUDDING

Simple, thrifty puddings were much loved, and were always prepared with care, using the best ingredients.

6 SERVINGS

3 cups whole milk
2 cups cream or half-and-half
1 teaspoon pure vanilla extract
½ cup sugar
a pinch of salt
½ cup short-grain rice
¼–½ teaspoon grated nutmeg
boiled cider syrup (page 135) to serve

Preheat the oven to 300°F.

Combine all the ingredients except the cider syrup in a buttered shallow baking dish and stir to mix. Bake 30 minutes, then stir the pudding. Bake 15 minutes longer, then stir again. Bake another 15 minutes and stir, then continue baking, without stirring, until the pudding is creamy and the top is golden brown, about 1½ hours longer. Cover the top with foil if it is browning too much.

Serve hot or at room temperature, with cider syrup.

COOK'S NOTE Use any combination of milk and cream you like, according to how rich you want the pudding to be.

BREAD PUDDING

Many Shaker recipes use "stale" bread. This was usually an extra loaf baked and kept a day. It might then be dried in the oven and coarsely ground by rolling to use as a crumb coating.

8 SERVINGS

2½ cups milk
4 tablespoons butter
½ cup sugar
1 teaspoon grated lemon zest
1 teaspoon pure vanilla extract
½ teaspoon ground cinnamon
5 cups slightly stale white bread without crusts, cut in cubes
¼ cup dried cherries
3 eggs, beaten
¼ cup chopped toasted pecans

FOR THE SAUCE

1 cup packed dark brown sugar
½ cup butter
¼ cup heavy cream

Combine the milk, butter and sugar in a heavy saucepan and heat, stirring to dissolve the sugar. Pour into a bowl. Stir in the lemon zest, vanilla and cinnamon. Add the bread cubes and cherries and stir to mix. Let soak 20 minutes.

Preheat the oven to 350°F.

Stir the eggs into the bread mixture. Add the pecans. Pour into a buttered shallow baking dish. Bake the pudding until it is set and golden brown on top, about 40 minutes.

Meanwhile, prepare the sauce. Combine the sugar and butter in a heavy saucepan and heat gently, stirring, to melt the butter and dissolve the sugar. Bring to a boil, then stir in the cream. Remove from the heat.

Serve the pudding hot, with the sauce.

COOK'S NOTE Use bread with a good texture if possible. If you prefer, serve the pudding with whipped cream or with sour cream and maple syrup.

BLUEBERRY CRISP

Blueberry bushes produced abundant fruit that was used in desserts such as cobblers and crisps or brown betties, as well as in pies and muffins.

4–6 SERVINGS

2 pints blueberries (4C)
½ C *1–2 tablespoons sugar*
1 teaspoon grated orange zest

FOR THE CRISP TOPPING

¾ cup flour
¾ cup packed light brown sugar
6 tablespoons butter, cut in pieces
½ cup rolled oats
½ teaspoon ground cinnamon

Preheat the oven to 350°F.

Combine the blueberries, sugar and orange zest and toss to mix. Put into a buttered shallow baking dish.

To make the topping, combine the flour, sugar and butter in a food processor and work just until the mixture resembles very coarse crumbs. (Turn the machine on and off a few times and take care not to process too finely.) Add the oats and cinnamon and process a few more seconds to blend.

Spread the topping mixture evenly over the fruit and pat down gently with your fingertips. Bake until the top is lightly browned and crisp, 35–40 minutes. Serve warm, with whipped cream or vanilla ice cream.

OVERLEAF: BLUEBERRY CRISP (LEFT), STRAWBERRY SHORTCAKE

CITRUS SPONGE PUDDING WITH CHERRY SAUCE

6 SERVINGS

4 tablespoons soft butter
⅔ cup sugar
1 tablespoon grated orange zest
1 teaspoon grated lemon zest
3 eggs, separated
¼ cup flour
¾ cup milk
½ cup orange juice
2 tablespoons lemon juice
a pinch of cream of tartar

FOR THE SAUCE

1½ cups fresh cherries, pitted
½ cup water
¼ cup orange juice
½ cup sugar

Preheat the oven to 350°F.

Beat the butter with the sugar, orange zest and lemon zest until very light and fluffy. Beat in the egg yolks and flour, then mix in the milk and juices. In another bowl, beat the egg whites until frothy. Add the cream of tartar and continue beating until soft peaks form. Add a large spoonful of the egg whites to the citrus mixture and beat in gently, then fold in the remaining whites.

Pour into a buttered 1-quart baking dish. Set the dish in a roasting pan containing hot water and bake until the pudding is golden brown and set and springs back when lightly pressed in the center, 40–45 minutes.

Meanwhile, make the sauce. Combine the cherries, water, orange juice and sugar in a saucepan and heat, stirring to dissolve the sugar. Bring to a boil and simmer 1 minute. With a slotted spoon remove the cherries from the pan and reserve. Continue boiling the liquid until it is reduced and syrupy. Return the cherries to the liquid and stir to mix. Set aside.

Serve the pudding hot with the warm cherry sauce.

STRAWBERRY SHORTCAKE

The large strawberry fields yielded basket upon basket of juicy, aromatic fruit, to make delicious jams and desserts. Strawberry shortcake was an early summer treat for Shaker Families.

6 SERVINGS

2 pints strawberries, hulled and sliced
½ cup sugar
1¼ cups heavy cream
1 teaspoon pure vanilla extract

FOR THE SHORTCAKE

2 cups flour
2½ teaspoons baking powder
¼ cup sugar
3 tablespoons butter
¼ cup vegetable shortening
⅓ cup half-and-half
1 egg, beaten

Put the strawberries in a bowl and sprinkle with half of the sugar. Toss gently. Cover and refrigerate.

Preheat the oven to 425°F.

To make the shortcake, sift the flour, baking powder and sugar into a bowl. Cut in the butter and shortening until the mixture resembles fine crumbs. Add the half-and-half and egg and mix quickly to a soft dough. Roll or pat out the dough to just over ½-inch thick and cut out six 3-inch rounds (take care not to twist the cutter). Set the rounds on an ungreased baking sheet, arranging them so they are nearly touching. Bake until well risen and golden brown, about 15 minutes. Transfer to a wire rack and let cool slightly.

Meanwhile, whip the cream until beginning to thicken. Add the remaining sugar and the vanilla and continue whipping until thick.

Split the warm shortcake rounds horizontally in half. Fill with the whipped cream and strawberries and serve immediately.

APPLE DUMPLINGS

To make maple sugar, the Shakers boiled the gallons of syrup they tapped from their trees until it was much reduced and concentrated. This syrup was beaten until it became creamy-brown in color, and it was poured into molds to set. The resulting maple sugar had a smooth texture (not crystalline like commercial granulated maple sugar), and it was shaved off to use in pies, cakes, cookies, puddings, and vegetable dishes.

4 SERVINGS

4 green apples, peeled
4 tablespoons granulated or shaved maple sugar
4 tablespoons heavy cream
2 tablespoons butter, cut in small pieces
³⁄₄ cup apple cider
¹⁄₂ cup pure maple syrup

FOR THE PASTRY

1¹⁄₂ cups flour
¹⁄₄ teaspoon salt
5 tablespoons cold butter, cut in pieces
¹⁄₄ cup vegetable shortening
3–4 tablespoons cold water

First make the pastry dough. Put the flour and salt in the food processor and turn the machine on briefly to blend. Add the butter and shortening and process until the mixture resembles coarse crumbs, turning the machine on and off several times. Add enough water to bind the ingredients (the mixture should still look crumbly). Turn onto the work surface and mix briefly with your hands to make a smooth dough. Gather into a ball, wrap and refrigerate 20 minutes.

Preheat the oven to 375°F.

Roll out the pastry dough thinly. Cut into four squares, each large enough to wrap an apple.

Using a small melon baller, remove the cores from the apples, working from the tops and keeping them whole. Do not cut all the way through. Put an apple in the center of each square of dough. Fill the hollow in each apple with maple sugar and cream and put the butter on top. Moisten the edges of the dough squares with water. Bring the corners of each square up over the top of the apple and press to seal; fold over and press all the edges to seal. Prick around the top of each dumpling with a fork to make a few steam vent holes.

Set the dumplings in a shallow baking pan and pour the cider and maple syrup around them. Bake until the apples are tender and the pastry is golden brown, about 45 minutes. Baste with the cider and syrup mixture every 15 minutes.

Serve the dumplings hot, with the pan juices.

SUMMER BERRY PUDDING

Fruits of all kinds were cultivated in Shaker fields and orchards, and the Brothers were always experimenting – grafting and testing new varieties. Kitchen Sisters had fresh fruits available almost all year round.

6 SERVINGS

2 pounds mixed berries, such as raspberries, blackberries, blueberries, strawberries and red or black currants
½ cup sugar
2–4 tablespoons blackberry cordial (page 142) or other fruit liqueur
8–12 slices of white bread, cut ½-inch thick, crusts trimmed

If using strawberries that are large, cut them in half or quarters so they are about the same size as the other berries. Put the berries in a heavy saucepan with the sugar. Cook over a low heat, stirring gently to dissolve the sugar, until the juices start to run from the fruit. Remove the pan from the heat and stir in the blackberry cordial.

Butter a 1- to 1½-quart mold and line the bottom with a disk of wax paper. Layer the bread and fruit in the mold, cutting the slices of bread to fit neatly and fill the gaps. Press each layer of fruit and bread firmly (without squashing the fruit too much). Start and finish with bread (make three or four layers of bread, according to taste). Moisten the top layer of bread with the fruit juices. Set a saucer or small plate on the bread and weight down (with a can of food, for example). Refrigerate overnight.

Unmold the pudding to serve, with cream.

BAKED PEACHES

The Shakers preferred to cook fruits and vegetables without peeling them, so that nothing would be wasted.

4 SERVINGS

soft butter
¼ cup packed granulated maple sugar or light brown sugar
4 ripe but firm peaches

Preheat the oven to 375°F.

Rub some soft butter over the bottom of a baking dish just large enough to accommodate 8 peach halves. Sprinkle the sugar evenly over the butter.

If you prefer, peel the peaches. Cut the peaches in half and remove the pits. Arrange the halves cut side down in the baking dish. Bake 10 minutes.

Turn the peach halves over and continue baking 5 minutes.

Serve hot or at room temperature, with ice cream, whipped cream or gingerbread (page 104).

ICED LEMON CREAM

The Shakers at North Union built an icehouse in 1874 to store the ice they cut from their lakes in winter. The ice could be kept for months, and then used in the summer to chill drinks, store food and freeze ice cream in the dairy.

MAKES JUST OVER 1 QUART

1 tablespoon grated lemon zest
⅔ cup fresh lemon juice
2 cups sugar
¼ cup water
3 cups heavy cream
1 cup half-and-half or milk

Combine the lemon zest and juice, sugar and water in a saucepan and bring to a boil, stirring to dissolve the sugar. Remove from the heat and let cool.

Mix together the cream and half-and-half or milk in a bowl. Strain in the lemon mixture and stir to mix. Pour into an ice cream churn (hand-cranked or electric) and freeze until firm.

BERRY WATER ICE

Among many Shaker kitchen inventions was a motorized ice cream freezer.

MAKES ABOUT 1 PINT

1 pound strawberries, raspberries or blackberries
¾–1 cup sugar
½ cup water
1–2 tablespoons lemon juice

Purée the berries with ¾ cup sugar in a food processor or blender. Add the water and 1 tablespoon lemon juice and process again until very smooth and the sugar has dissolved. Pass the purée through a fine nylon strainer, pressing firmly with a rubber spatula. Taste and add more sugar and/or lemon juice: the mixture should be highly flavored.

In cooking, and the general labor of the dining-room and kitchen, the sisters take turns; a certain number, sufficient to make the work light, serving a month at a time...Their diet is simple but efficient.

CHARLES NORDHOFF
THE COMMUNISTIC SOCIETIES OF THE UNITED STATES, 1875

Pour into an ice cream churn (hand-cranked or electric) and freeze until firm. Or, still freeze in a container, whisking several times to prevent large ice crystals forming.

ROSEWATER ICE CREAM

At one time, it was forbidden for flowers to be grown simply for their beauty and scent – they had to have a function, culinary or medicinal. Roses were cultivated only for the making of rosewater, which was used as a flavoring as well as to cure fever. These strict rules were relaxed in the late nineteenth century.

MAKES ABOUT 1 QUART

2 cups heavy cream
1 cup light cream
1 cup milk
¾ cup sugar
6 egg yolks
1 tablespoon rosewater or more to taste

Put 1 cup of the cream and the milk in a heavy saucepan and heat until bubbles appear around the edge. Add the sugar and heat almost to boiling point, stirring to dissolve the sugar.

Lightly beat the egg yolks in a bowl. Slowly add the hot cream mixture to the yolks, stirring constantly. Pour back into the pan (or into the top of a double boiler, if you prefer) and cook over medium-low heat, stirring, until the custard thickens enough to coat the spoon thinly. Do not boil.

Strain the custard into a bowl or pitcher and stir in the remaining cream and rosewater to taste (the mixture should be highly flavored). Pour into an ice cream churn (hand-cranked or electric) and freeze until firm.

COOK'S NOTE For a less rich ice cream use 2 cups each cream and milk.

OVERLEAF: ROSEWATER ICE CREAM (LEFT), MAPLE PECAN FUDGE

RHUBARB AND STRAWBERRY PIE

Shaker Sisters were always baking pies, with fillings chosen according to the season: soft fruits in spring and summer; squash, sweet potatoes and cranberries in the fall; mincemeat and other preserved fruits in winter. A revolving oven, designed by Eldress Emeline Hart at Canterbury in 1876, could accommodate dozens of pies or loaves of bread at the same time.

8 OR MORE SERVINGS

1 pound rhubarb, cut in 1-inch pieces
(3 heaped cups)
14 ounces strawberries, hulled and sliced
(2 heaped cups)
2 tablespoons flour or instant tapioca
½ cup granulated sugar plus extra for sprinkling
½ cup packed light brown sugar
1 tablespoon butter, cut in small flakes
light cream

FOR THE PIECRUST

2 cups flour
½ teaspoon salt
⅓ cup vegetable shortening
4 tablespoons cold butter, cut in pieces
1 egg yolk lightly beaten with 3 tablespoons cold water
soft butter

To make the piecrust dough, put the flour and salt in the food processor and turn the machine on briefly to blend. Add the shortening and butter and process until the mixture resembles coarse crumbs, turning the machine on and off several times. Add the egg yolk mixture to bind the ingredients (the mixture should still look crumbly). Turn onto the work surface and mix briefly with your hands to make a smooth dough. Gather into a ball, wrap and refrigerate 20 minutes.

Preheat the oven to 375°F.

Divide the dough into two portions, one slightly larger than the other. Roll out the larger portion and use to line a 9-inch pie plate. Brush a film of soft butter over the bottom.

Combine the rhubarb, strawberries, flour or tapioca and sugars in a bowl and toss gently to mix well. Pour into the piecrust and spread out evenly, doming the fruit slightly in the center. Dot with the flakes of butter. Roll out the remaining dough, cut in strips and use to make a lattice top. Brush the strips lightly with cream and sprinkle them with sugar.

Bake the pie until the pastry is golden brown and the fruit filling is juicy and tender, about 45 minutes. Cover the piecrust edge with foil if it is browning too much. Set the pie plate on a wire rack to cool.

COOK'S NOTE If the strawberries are very ripe and the rhubarb is likely to be juicy, you may need more flour or tapioca.

APPLE PIE

Apple pie, with its traditional flavoring of rosewater, was a Shaker favorite, and according to the season the pie would be made with fresh or dried apples. The orchards were very large, and huge quantities of apples were cut and dried every fall. Even the children helped in the preparation.

8 OR MORE SERVINGS

pastry for a double-crust pie
(page 127, Lemon Pie)
6 cups peeled, cored and thinly sliced apples
¾ cup sugar (or more according to the sweetness of the apples) plus extra for sprinkling
2 tablespoons heavy cream
1 tablespoon rosewater

Preheat the oven to 375°F.

Divide the dough into two portions, one slightly larger than the other. Roll out the larger portion and use to line a 9-inch pie plate.

Combine the apple slices, sugar, cream and rosewater in a bowl and mix well together. Tip into the piecrust and spread out evenly. Roll out the remaining dough for the top crust and crimp the edges to seal. Cut a few slits in the top crust as steam vent holes. Brush the crust lightly with water and sprinkle with sugar.

Bake the pie until the pastry is golden brown and the apples are tender, about 45 minutes. Cover the piecrust edge with foil if it is browning too much. Set the pie plate on a wire rack to cool.

LEMON PIE

Rich lemon pie like this was traditionally made by the Ohio and Kentucky Shakers, but recipes for lemon pies of all kinds appear in the diaries and handwritten cookbooks of all Shaker communities.

8 OR MORE SERVINGS

2 large or 3 medium-size juicy lemons, well scrubbed
about 2 cups sugar
soft butter
4 eggs

FOR THE PIECRUST

2 cups flour
½ teaspoon salt
¼ cup vegetable shortening
6–8 tablespoons cold butter, cut in pieces
1 egg yolk lightly beaten with 3 tablespoons cold
water

Cut the lemons into paper-thin slices, then quarter the slices. Remove any seeds and discard the end slices.

Layer the lemon slices in a bowl, sprinkling with 2 cups of sugar. Cover the bowl and let stand several hours, or overnight if more convenient.

To make the piecrust dough, put the flour and salt in the food processor and turn the machine on briefly to blend. Add the shortening and butter and process until the mixture resembles coarse crumbs, turning the machine on and off several times. Add the egg yolk mixture to bind the ingredients (the mixture should still look crumbly). Turn onto the work surface and mix briefly with your hands to make a smooth dough. Gather into a ball, wrap and refrigerate 20 minutes.

Preheat the oven to 375°F.

Divide the dough into two portions, one slightly larger than the other. Roll out the larger portion and use to line a 9-inch pie plate. Brush the bottom of the piecrust with a film of soft butter.

Lift the lemon slices out of the bowl and layer them in the pie crust. Sprinkle with a little more sugar if desired. Add the eggs to the sugary lemon juice in the bowl and beat until well blended. Pour over the lemon slices. Roll out the remaining dough for the top crust and crimp the edges to seal. Cut a few slits in the top crust as steam vent holes.

Bake the pie until the pastry is golden brown, about 45 minutes. Cover the piecrust edge with foil if it is browning too much. Set the pie plate on a wire rack to cool.

COOK'S NOTE Use only half of the lemon slices in the pie, if you prefer.

OVERLEAF: LEMON PIE

PEACH AND APRICOT LEATHER

The delicious sweetmeat called fruit leather was one of many ways to use up dried fruits. Leathers could be sweetened with sugar or honey.

MAKES ABOUT 10 OUNCES

¼ pound dried apricots
¼ pound dried peaches
1½ cups water
½ cup sugar
confectioners' sugar

Combine the apricots, peaches and water in a saucepan. Bring to a boil, then remove from the heat. Cover and let soak overnight.

The next day, bring back to a boil and simmer, covered, until the fruit is very soft and pulpy, 30–35 minutes. Let cool slightly, then purée in a blender or food processor. Add the sugar and blend until completely dissolved. Return the purée to the pan and continue cooking, uncovered, over low heat until the fruit mixture is very thick and excess liquid has evaporated, 10–20 minutes longer. When done, a spoon drawn through the mixture will leave a clear channel on the bottom of the pan. Stir frequently during cooking to be sure the mixture doesn't stick. Remove from the heat and let cool slightly.

Turn onto 2 large baking sheets lined with wax paper or baking parchment and spread out evenly with a spatula to very thin sheets. Let cool and dry; when ready the leather should no longer feel tacky to the touch.

Cut the leather into strips and dust with confectioners' sugar to prevent the strips sticking together.

COOK'S NOTE Drying can take 1–2 days depending on the moisture in the air. You can speed things by drying in an oven on a very low setting.

MAPLE PECAN FUDGE

In the early spring, when the snow is still on the ground, the sap starts to rise in the maple tree; then it is time for "sugaring off" to make maple syrup, an event greatly anticipated in Shaker communities.

MAKES ABOUT 80 PIECES

1½ cups sugar
1½ cups pure maple syrup
1 cup heavy cream
¼ teaspoon salt
¼ teaspoon cream of tartar
2 cups coarsely chopped pecans or other nuts
1 teaspoon pure vanilla extract

Butter the sides of a heavy deep saucepan. Put the sugar, maple syrup, cream, salt and cream of tartar in the pan and heat, stirring to dissolve the sugar. Once dissolved, stop stirring and bring to a boil. Boil to the soft ball stage (240°F on a candy thermometer).

Meanwhile, spread the nuts evenly in a buttered 9-inch square pan.

Remove the saucepan from the heat and let the bubbles subside, then stir in the vanilla. Let cool to 110°F, then beat with a wooden spoon until the mixture starts to thicken and look creamy. Quickly pour into the buttered pan over the nuts (do not scrape out the saucepan). Let cool, then cut in 1-inch squares. Best freshly made.

COOK'S NOTE Unless you are an experienced candy maker, it is best to use a candy thermometer.

MOLASSES CREAM TAFFY

In the late nineteenth century, parties called taffy pulls were very popular among young people. The Shakers, too, enjoyed the fun of stretching the candy, and they invented a taffy hook to help.

MAKES ABOUT 1 POUND

1 cup light molasses
1 cup sugar
2 teaspoons vinegar
½ cup light cream
2 tablespoons butter, cut in small flakes
confectioners' sugar

Butter the sides of a heavy saucepan. Combine the molasses, sugar and vinegar in the pan and heat gently, stirring to dissolve the sugar. Once the sugar has dissolved, stop stirring, increase the heat and bring the mixture to a boil. Boil to the soft ball stage (240°F on a sugar thermometer).

Gradually stir in the cream, then add the butter, a few pieces at a time. Bring back to a boil, without stirring, and boil over medium heat to just over the soft crack stage (265–270°F).

Pour the hot syrup slowly onto a lightly buttered heat-proof surface or into a lightly buttered pan (do not scrape the saucepan). Let cool 2–3 minutes, then begin working the syrup with a candy scraper, turning and pushing it into a mass in the center of the pan. When it is cool enough to handle, start working the taffy with buttered fingers (not your whole hand), pulling it out as far as it will stretch and then folding it back on itself. Continue the pulling and folding until the taffy starts to firm and is no longer sticky. Then add twisting to the pulling and folding. The taffy is ready when it is opaque and firm yet elastic.

Pull it into a twisted rope about 1-inch thick and let it fall onto wax paper. Snip into pieces with buttered scissors. When they are cool, toss the pieces of taffy in confectioners' sugar to prevent them sticking together and store in an airtight tin, or wrap them individually in wax paper.

COOK'S NOTE Work with batches that you can comfortably hold. Try to pull the taffy in a cool place: if the room is warm and humid, the pulling can take up to 20 minutes.

SPRING WAS THE TIME TO FORM MAPLE SUGAR CANDIES, SHOWN HERE AT CANTERBURY SHAKER VILLAGE

CHAPTER SEVEN

PRESERVES, SAUCES AND BEVERAGES

Vast quantities of canned and dried fruits and vegetables, plus pickles, relishes, jams and other preserves, were prepared throughout the growing season for the winter stores as well as to sell to the World. Applesauce, in particular, was made in such bulk that it was eaten at every meal. Apples were also pressed into cider, which was a favorite beverage together with fruit wines and herbal teas.

CORN RELISH

Pickles, relishes and sauces enlivened the simply prepared food on Shaker tables, and provided variety during the winter months.

MAKES ABOUT 3 PINTS

8 ears of corn
1 large white onion, minced
1 red bell pepper, seeded and diced
1 green bell pepper, seeded and diced
2 celery stalks, diced
½ small head green cabbage
(about ½ pound), finely chopped
1 cup sugar
1¼ cups cider vinegar
½ cup water
2 teaspoons mustard seeds
½ teaspoon turmeric
½ tablespoon salt

Shuck the corn. With a sharp knife, cut the kernels from the cobs. You should have about 4 cups of kernels.

Put the corn in a large non-reactive kettle or pan and add the remaining ingredients. Bring just to a boil, stirring to dissolve the sugar. Simmer 30 minutes, stirring occasionally.

Pack in hot sterilized jars, leaving ½-inch headspace. Cover and process in a boiling water bath 15 minutes.

CRANBERRY CATSUP

Shaker cooks ground their own spices, using a mill or a mortar and pestle, so they were always fresh and fragrant.

MAKES ABOUT 2 PINTS

1 quart cranberries
1 onion, minced
2 cups packed light brown sugar, or 1 cup white and
1 cup brown sugar
1 cup cider vinegar
1 cup water
1 teaspoon salt
½ teaspoon pepper
1 teaspoon ground allspice
½ teaspoon ground mace

Combine all the ingredients in a non-reactive kettle or pot. Bring just to a boil, stirring to dissolve the sugar. Reduce the heat and simmer gently until the cranberries are very tender and pulped, about 45 minutes.

Let cool slightly, then ladle into a food processor and work until quite smooth. Press through a strainer into a clean pan.

Bring the catsup back to a boil. If necessary, simmer until thickened to a catsup consistency, stirring occasionally. (Keep watching to be sure the catsup doesn't thicken too much and turn into a jam!)

Pack into hot sterilized bottles and seal.

SPICED PICKLED PEARS

It was common for each of the Families in a Shaker community to have its own fruit orchards, growing pears, peaches, apples, plums, cherries and quinces, according to climate.

2 cups sugar
2½ cups distilled white vinegar or half white and half cider vinegar
2½ cups water
6 cinnamon sticks
2 tablespoons whole cloves
1 tablespoon black peppercorns
3 pounds small firm pears

Combine the sugar, vinegar and water in a large non-reactive kettle or pot. Add the spices. Bring to a boil, stirring to dissolve the sugar. Boil 5 minutes. Remove from the heat.

Peel the pears. Core them from the base, using a melon baller or small knife, so that they stay whole. Add the pears to the spiced syrup as they are prepared.

Bring the syrup back to a boil, then reduce the heat and simmer until the pears are tender but still firm.

Remove the pears with a slotted spoon and pack into a hot sterilized jar that is just large enough to accommodate them (1 to 1½ quart). Boil the syrup until it is reduced to about 2 cups. Strain the syrup. Add a few of the spices to the jar, then pour the syrup over the pears to fill the jar. Seal and process in a boiling water bath 5 minutes.

COOK'S NOTE If you prefer, tie the spices in a cheesecloth bag.

BOILED CIDER SYRUP

Shaker boiled cider was made by slowly boiling freshly pressed apple cider until it had reduced to about one-quarter of the original volume. It was used as a flavoring, and as a sweetener in place of sugar.

MAKES ABOUT 1½ CUPS

2 quarts apple cider
1 cinnamon stick, broken in half
a few whole cloves
¾–1 cup sugar

Put the cider and spices in a large wide pan and bring to a boil. Skim off the foam that rises to the surface. Boil the cider until it has reduced to about 2 cups.

Add sugar to taste (according to the sweetness of the apples used to make the cider) and stir until it has dissolved. Continue boiling until the cider is just syrupy: take a little on a teaspoon, cool and tilt the spoon to see how the syrup runs.

Strain the syrup and pour it into a sterilized bottle.

COOK'S NOTE The spiced tart-sweet syrup can be served with desserts such as rice pudding, baked custard and bread pudding, and used to baste pork chops and ham slices.

OVERLEAF: CRANBERRY CATSUP (LEFT), APPLESAUCE

HERB VINEGARS

The early Shakers learned about wild herbs and roots from the Native Americans, and they transplanted both culinary and medicinal herbs to their gardens to cultivate. As a result Shaker Sisters had many different herbs available for cooking as well as to make teas and herbal medicines. In time, the selling of dried herbs became the chief source of income for many Shaker communities as an entry in a journal dated March 7, 1845, indicates: "Elisha has finished printing between seventy and eighty thousand labels for herbs."

sprigs of fresh herbs, such as mint, tarragon, rosemary, thyme, sage, basil, bay, fennel, chives, marjoram or dill
mild white or cider vinegar (use only white vinegar for mint)

Put the lightly crushed herb sprigs (one kind or a mixture) in a sterilized bottle. Warm the vinegar and pour it over the herbs. Seal and let stand 2–3 weeks.

Strain the vinegar, pressing all liquid from the herbs. Discard the herbs. Put fresh herb sprigs in the bottle and pour in the vinegar. Seal again and keep in a cool dark place.

COOK'S NOTE If you prefer, use wine vinegar.

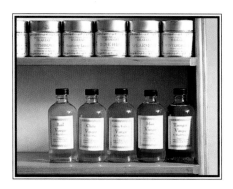

APPLE BUTTER

Applesauce and apple butter were made in quantity every fall, and the Shaker-invented machine that pared, cored and quartered or sliced apples no doubt made the job much faster and easier.

MAKES ABOUT 2 PINTS

1 quart apple cider
3 pounds tart cooking apples, peeled, cored and chopped
1 cup packed light brown sugar
1 cup packed dark brown sugar
2 teaspoons ground cinnamon
1 teaspoon ground allspice
1 teaspoon ground ginger

Put the cider in a heavy kettle or other large deep pot and bring to a boil. Boil until reduced to 1 cup, skimming the surface occasionally.

Add the apples to the cider. Cover and simmer until the apples are very soft and pulpy, 15–20 minutes.

Remove from the heat and mash the apples until smooth, or purée in a food processor or blender and return to the pot.

Add the sugars and spices and stir to dissolve the sugar. Simmer very gently until very thick, about 45 minutes longer. When ready, you should be able to draw a spoon through the apple butter, leaving a clear channel on the bottom of the pot that slowly fills up. Stir frequently during cooking to prevent the apple butter from sticking to the pot, and part cover the pot if necessary as the apple butter spatters a lot as it bubbles.

Ladle into hot sterilized jars and seal.

COOK'S NOTE Use well-flavored apples such as Jonathan or Winesap.

APPLESAUCE

Shaker applesauce was traditionally made from boiled cider and from either fresh apples or soaked dried apples. The pieces of apple remained whole in the rich syrup. Applesauce was sold to the World for over 50 years.

MAKES ABOUT 2 PINTS

1½ quarts hard apple cider
2 pounds tart green apples, peeled, cored and sliced
sugar to taste, brown or white
lemon juice to taste

Pour the cider into a kettle or other large wide pot and bring to a boil. Skim the foam from the surface. Boil until reduced to 1½ cups.

Add the apple slices, cover and simmer gently until they are tender but still firm, about 10 minutes. With a slotted spoon, remove the apple slices. Pack in hot sterilized jars if you are intending to keep the applesauce; otherwise, transfer to a bowl.

Sweeten the cider to taste and boil until it is a little syrupy. Add a squeeze or two of lemon juice to sharpen the flavor, then pour the syrup over the apples. Serve warm or cold.

COOK'S NOTES If you can't get hard cider, substitute sweet cider or unsweetened apple juice. Depending on the apples used to make the cider or juice, and how sweet you like applesauce, you may not need much sugar. If you prefer a smooth applesauce, you can mash the apples before mixing in the syrupy cider.

SHAKER APPLE SAUCE

Address **D. C. BRAINARD,** MT. LEBANON, COL., CO., N.Y.

····• PACKED AT •····

A JAR LABEL SHOWING THE SHAKERS' MASTERY OF EYE-CATCHING DESIGN

Fragrant puffs of boiling fruit and spices emanated from the basement kitchen and filled the halls — perhaps they were making apple sauce that day. The odor suggested it.

WRITTEN BY A VISITOR TO SABBATHDAY LAKE IN 1910, QUOTED IN
THE FOUR SEASONS OF SHAKER LIFE BY GERARD C. WERTKIN

OVERLEAF: HERB VINEGARS

RASPBERRY SHRUB

The original shrubs, from colonial days, were fermented alcoholic drinks. In 1828, the Shaker central ministry forbade strong drink in all communities, and thereafter the much-enjoyed hard cider had to be left to sour into vinegar.

MAKES 3½–4 CUPS

1 quart raspberries
½ cup mild cider vinegar
sugar
still or sparkling water

Put the berries in a large non-reactive bowl and crush lightly with a fork or potato masher. Add the vinegar and stir to mix. Cover and let stand 24 hours.

Strain the juice, rubbing as much of the pulp through the strainer as possible. Measure the juice. To each cup add a cup of sugar. Put into a saucepan and heat, stirring to dissolve the sugar. Bring just to a boil.

Pour the syrup into hot sterilized bottles. Keep in the refrigerator, and use within 3–4 weeks.

To serve, dilute one part syrup with three or four parts still or sparkling water and pour over crushed ice.

COOK'S NOTE If you want to keep the raspberry syrup longer than 3–4 weeks, you can boil it before bottling; this will prevent it fermenting. However, boiling the syrup will lessen its very fresh flavor.

BLACKBERRY CORDIAL

Fruit cordials were prepared as medicinal drinks, and they were given to the sick and elderly.

MAKES ABOUT 1½ PINTS

1 quart ripe blackberries
2 cinnamon sticks
1 teaspoon whole cloves
1 teaspoon whole allspice
about 1 cup sugar
1 cup brandy or cognac

Purée the blackberries in a blender or food processor, then press the purée through a fine nylon strainer. Put the resulting blackberry juice in a saucepan and add the spices. Sweeten the juice with sugar to taste. Bring just to a boil, stirring to dissolve the sugar, then simmer gently about 5 minutes.

Strain the blackberry syrup and let cool. When cold, stir in the brandy or cognac. Store in tightly stoppered bottles. Serve neat or mix with soda; or add a spoonful to a glass of white or sparkling wine.

COOK'S NOTE For a very smooth cordial, strain the blackberry purée through a piece of cheesecloth, squeezing to extract all the juice.

GINGERADE

Thirst-quenching beverages were prepared in hot weather to take to the workers in the fields. Ginger was much used for spicing the drinks – in quantities that would probably not be palatable to us today.

4–6 SERVINGS

1½–2 tablespoons minced fresh ginger
½ tablespoon grated lemon zest
5 cups boiling water
2 tablespoons freshly squeezed lemon juice or more to taste
4 tablespoons mild honey or more to taste

Put the ginger and lemon zest in a pitcher and pour in the boiling water. Stir, then let steep about 1 hour.

Strain the liquid. Stir in the lemon juice and honey. Taste and add more lemon juice or honey if desired. Serve chilled.

HERBADE

Shaker journals contain many recipes for delicious beverages, both hot and cold.

6 SERVINGS

½ cup sugar
1 cup water
1 cup coarsely chopped fresh mint leaves
½ cup coarsely chopped fresh bee balm (lemon balm) leaves
½ cup freshly squeezed lemon juice
½ cup freshly squeezed orange juice
1 quart chilled sparkling water

Put the sugar and water in a saucepan and bring to a boil, stirring to dissolve the sugar. Boil the syrup about 5 minutes. Let cool slightly.

Combine the herbs, sugar syrup and juices in a bowl and stir well to mix. Cover and let stand at least 1 hour, mashing the herbs with a fork or spoon now and then.

Strain the mixture into a pitcher, pressing the herbs to extract all liquid. Just before serving, stir in the sparkling water. Serve over ice.

COOK'S NOTE If you do not have any bee balm growing in your garden, use 1½ cups mint (preferably different varieties) and add 1 tablespoon grated lemon zest.

OVERLEAF: LEFT TO RIGHT – GINGERADE, HERBADE, RASPBERRY SHRUB

CLACKETY TRACK

CLACKETY TRACK

POEMS ABOUT TRAINS

Skila Brown   illustrated by Jamey Christoph

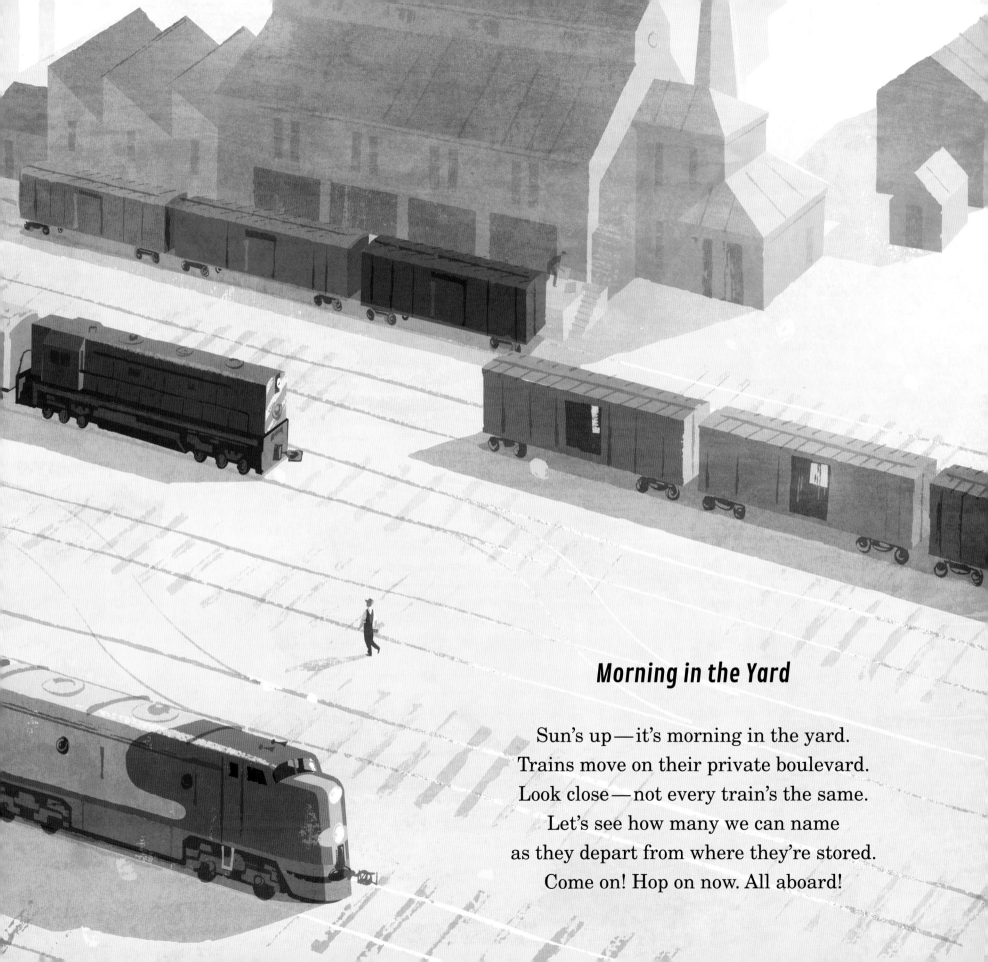

Morning in the Yard

Sun's up—it's morning in the yard.
Trains move on their private boulevard.
Look close—not every train's the same.
Let's see how many we can name
as they depart from where they're stored.
Come on! Hop on now. All aboard!

Freight Train

There's nothin' plain about a train.
White-striped engines lead the chain.

Cars—curved and straight. Open. Enclosed.
Pallet piles and logs exposed.

Clankin' crayon pack on wheels.
Racin' rainbow made of steel.

Rows of grooves, cables, and bars.
Graffiti rockin' out the cars.

A badge of rust. A proud oil stain.
There's nothin' plain about a train.

Tracks

Stretched web path.

No start. No end.

Crisscross the ground

around a bend.

Wood ties. Steel beams.

Locked tight. Secure.

Around—things move.

Tracks stay. Endure.

Tracks wait to see

which train will come.

A s h u d d e r felt.

Hiss of brake drum.

Start of a song.

Click-clack refrain.

Listen.   Hush.

Here comes a train.

Bullet Train

jet-train   sleek and slick

      land-plane   quick. quick. quick.

faster than a cheetah
racing down a hill

    step up close and brace for
    a whoosh-y, windblown thrill

Steam Engine

Biggest beast you've ever seen.
Gobbling up a coal cuisine.
One hundred tons of steel machine.
Belching out a steam smoke screen.

Train Snow Plow

Keep back from the tracks
when the snow plow's coming.
Whatever you do—steer clear.

With its nose to the ground,
it comes pushing and humming.
Give a wave to the brave engineer.

It side-slings the snow
like a thick fountain sprayed.
All around it, the crowd gives a cheer.

But don't get too close
to the train plow's cascade.
If you do, you might disappear.

Zoo Train

Get your ticket and your snacks. This is the train for you.
You can look for weasel packs and watch the hippos chew.
Tigers lying on their backs and piles of rhino poo!
The only tracks close to yaks—it's such a perfect view.
This is where your legs relax, riding the train at the zoo.

Electric Train

Power from the wire.

Pantograph required.

Cabled Line of Fire.

Tethered Train Flyer.

Dinner Train

You tell the crew,
"Table for two,"
unpack your appetite.

You sip and chew,
drink in the view;
the sunset's such a sight.

Try something new . . .
Goat stew? Fondue?
Hot cocoa sounds quite right.

A smile for you
from bread up to
the last dessert-y bite.

The Underground Train

Deeper than the moles dig, the worms dig, the mice dig,
Deeper than the rats dig is the Underground Train.

It's filled with announcement sounds, beeping sounds, doors-closing sounds,
The clanking and the braking sounds—the squeal and the strain.

It travels through with pipes above, rocks above, homes above.
Traffic's stopped on streets above as it zooms along.

People go below the ground, work-bound, home-bound,
People flowing up and down, an all-day steady throng.

Inside the cars are laughing people, sleeping people, reading people.
Workers, babies, older people ride it every day.

Underneath the smog-filled streets, the crowded streets, the sizzling streets,
Deep below the stop-still streets is the cool subway.

churn around SLOSH CLEAN SPIT MUD OUT THE SIDE!

What a dusty ride!

Whistle-Stop Tour

Opulent train, regal and grand,
Each stop is brief, already planned,
Rolls into town, someone strikes up the band,
The whistle-stop tour, the whistle-stop tour.

The leader walks out to the balcony stand,
Says a few words, the crowd gives a hand,
Then the train pulls away, travels over the land.
The whistle-stop tour, the whistle-stop tour.

Sleeper Train

Hush.

      Here comes a train.
Open the walls and pull the beds down.
Climb up and slide in and don't move around.
Hook on the sleep straps and slip right through town.
      Hush.
    Here comes a train.

       Hush.
         Here comes a train.
      Chuggety, hufflety snuggle down deep,
      Clackety, trackety counting of sheep,
      Clinkety, rockety, sleepity sleep.
        Hush.
       Here comes a train.

Train Facts

The largest steam locomotives were built in the 1940s. The Union Pacific Big Boys, for example, were so massive they could haul 100 full wagons, traveling as fast as 70 miles/110 kilometers per hour.

Extra locomotives, called distributed-power units, can be placed between or behind freight cars on very long trains to help them haul long, heavy loads without derailing.

Engineers don't just drive the train; they also have to inspect all its mechanical aspects and keep an eye on the speed, brakes, and gauges.

Ballast is the crushed stone around train tracks that helps distribute the weight of the train, prevents plants from growing on the tracks, and gives snow and rain a way to drain.

Conductors are responsible for all things related to the safety of the train. They monitor the loading and unloading of freight and passengers, supervise the train crew, and keep the train on schedule.

Some railway tunnels are short (there's one in Tennessee that's only 46 feet/14 meters long), and some are very long (there's one under the Swiss Alps that goes for 35 miles/55 kilometers).

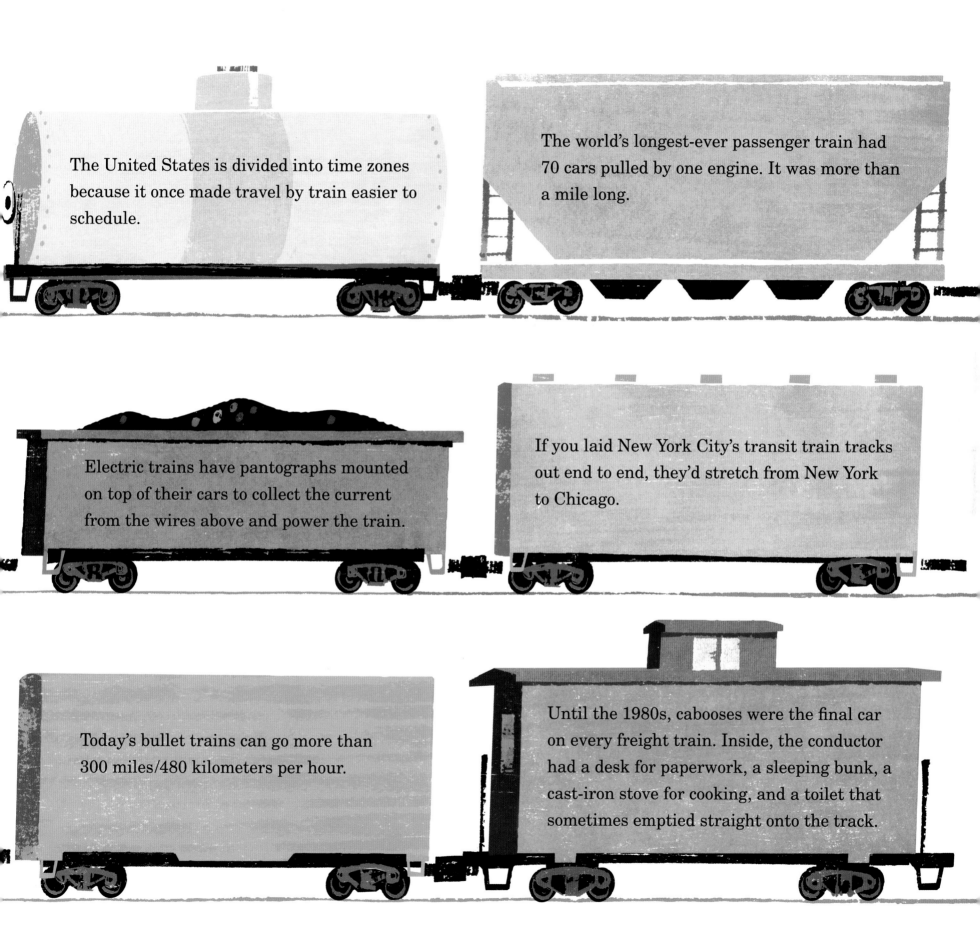

The United States is divided into time zones because it once made travel by train easier to schedule.

The world's longest-ever passenger train had 70 cars pulled by one engine. It was more than a mile long.

Electric trains have pantographs mounted on top of their cars to collect the current from the wires above and power the train.

If you laid New York City's transit train tracks out end to end, they'd stretch from New York to Chicago.

Today's bullet trains can go more than 300 miles/480 kilometers per hour.

Until the 1980s, cabooses were the final car on every freight train. Inside, the conductor had a desk for paperwork, a sleeping bunk, a cast-iron stove for cooking, and a toilet that sometimes emptied straight onto the track.

For Luís—who kept this one on track
S. B.

For Grandpa—who was happiest down by the tracks
on the lookout for passing trains
J. C.

First edition 2019

Library of Congress Catalog Card Number pending
ISBN 978-0-7636-9047-2

18 19 20 21 22 23 CCP 10 9 8 7 6 5 4 3 2 1

Printed in Shenzhen, Guangdong, China

This book was typeset in New Century Schoolbook.
The illustrations were created digitally.

Candlewick Press
99 Dover Street
Somerville, Massachusetts 02144

visit us at www.candlewick.com

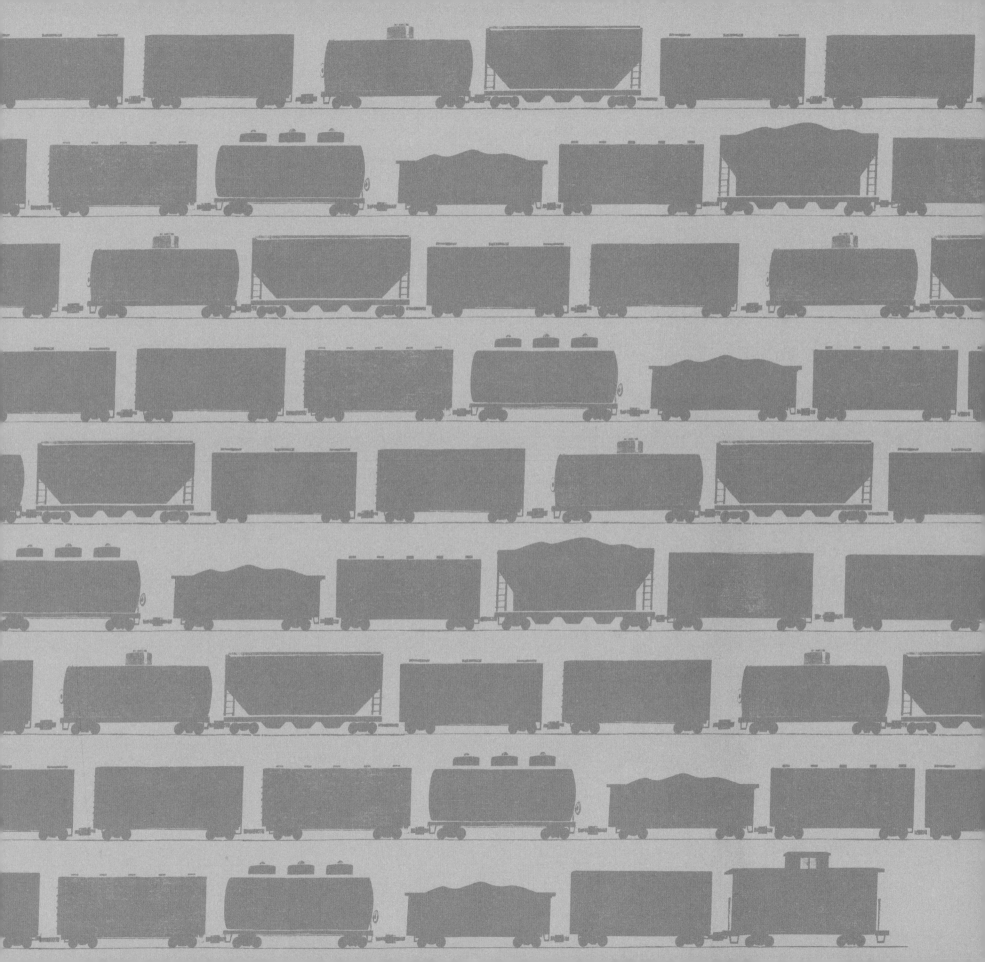